THE IMPASSE OF
MODERNITY

ABOUT THE AUTHOR

CHRISTIAN COMELIAU is an economist. Since 1990 he has been Professor of Development Economics at the Institute of Development Studies (IUED) in Geneva. Prior to this he held a variety of posts, which include teaching at the National University of Zaïre, Kinshasa, working as an economist at the World Bank, Washington DC, and subsequently at the OECD's Development Centre in Paris. He has also served as *chargé de mission* at the French planning agency, the Commissariat Général du Plan. He is the author of several well-regarded books in French.

THE IMPASSE OF
MODERNITY

Debating the Future of the
Global Market Economy

CHRISTIAN COMELIAU

Translated by
Patrick Camiller

ZED BOOKS
London & New York

FERNWOOD PUBLISHING LTD
Halifax, Nova Scotia

The Impasse of Modernity was first published in French
under the title *Les impasses de la modernité* in 2000
and in English in 2002 by
Zed Books Ltd, 7 Cynthia Street, London N1 9JF, UK,
and Room 400, 175 Fifth Avenue, New York, NY 10010, USA

Published in Canada by Fernwood Publishing Ltd,
PO Box 9409, Station A, Halifax, Nova Scotia, Canada B3K 5S3

Distributed in the USA exclusively by Palgrave, a division of
St Martin's Press, LLC, 175 Fifth Avenue, New York, NY 10010, USA

Copyright © Éditions du Seuil 2000
Translation copyright © Patrick Camiller 2002

The translation of this work was funded in part as a result of the
generous financial support of the Institut Universitaire d'Études
du Developpement (IUED) in Geneva.

The right of Christian Comeliau to be identified as the author
of this work has been asserted by him in accordance with the Copyright,
Designs and Patents Act, 1988

Designed and typeset in Bembo by Illuminati, Grosmont
Cover designed by Andrew Corbett
Printed and bound in Malaysia

A catalogue record for this book is available from the British Library
Library of Congress Cataloging-in-Publication Data applied for
National Library of Canada Cataloguing in Publication Data applied for

ISBN 1 85649 985 5 (Hb)
ISBN 1 85649 986 3 (Pb)

In Canada
ISBN 1 55266 068 0 (Pb)

CONTENTS

PREFACE

We live at a time when triumphant liberalism shows no restraint in proclaiming the virtues of globalization. Yet on this planet of ours, shaken by tragedies and absurdities, we can see a profound disquiet gradually expressing itself in the face of manifold social and economic contradictions, as the costs for society continue to mount and the sense that no one controls the direction of change becomes ever more distinct.

I said this planet of ours, rather than French or European societies, or the North as opposed to the South and vice versa. For although we have yet to see the rapid homogenization that is supposed to be carrying all the continents towards the same type of material progress, globalization does denote a reality in which powerful forces impose the same constraints and opportunities of 'modernity' upon societies — societies that are, and will remain, different.

The growth of this unease with modernity is a major event of our times. It is mainly felt — or ought to be mainly felt — not by specialists, of whatever description, but by ordinary citizens. If modernity disturbs them, our explanation for this should not remain at the surface, but should uncover the underlying reasons and the most important mechanisms of the overall system of modernity. Such an analytic effort entails rigorous use of the instruments of social science, for these are evidently in the front line of any account of the new sense of disquiet. My own contribution will be based on some economic reflections about the system of modernity as a whole, and the 'model of development' that it spreads. But reflections about this model cannot consist merely of an economist's analysis of the economy, as if all the complementary aspects could be left up to other disciplines to elaborate. Economics could be just one branch of the social sciences among others, but it is not content with such a place, and claims to be supreme in the influence it exerts on society. The kind of analysis we need might therefore be described, a little ambitiously perhaps, as 'meta-economics': a mode of thought which, though it rests upon the concepts and cognitive acquisitions of economic science, raises itself one stage higher to study their influence on values and cultures, on the use of natural resources, and even on political organization. The adoption of this vantage point will thus involve an attempt to put economics back in its rightful place.

Nor is this all. For the main point is not to open an academic discussion of these issues, but to pave the way collectively for a political debate in society at large. Without giving up a world-system perspective, or insistence on rigorous analysis, it will be necessary to present the essential points in terms that are accessible to all – that is, not to rest content with more or less scholarly theoretical constructions, but to look for results at the level of specific proposals and innovative social practices.

The chief aim of this book, then, is to link up interdisciplinary reflection with the groundwork for a crucial political debate. But to say this is also to highlight the difficulties of the undertaking. First of all, the 'experts' who govern our affairs have a sovereign disdain for anything that escapes their own special field: for them, a global approach is synonymous with unavowed incompetence, and they often prefer to criticize everyone and remain misunderstood, rather than accept all the risks of dialogue. A graver difficulty, however, stems from the ambitiousness of the 'overall vision' itself, which claims not only to draw upon specialized research but also to go beyond it by showing how the various observable facts and tendencies are related to one another. Let us venture a somewhat trivial comparison: an overall vision involves a method that is the opposite of the one used in television news; it refuses to list the facts in order that they can be described and interpreted separately; it seeks to demonstrate that the facts may be linked to one another, or linked to a more general explanation; it tries to draw out and analyse those links; it shows, for example, that one cannot at one and the same time call for the state to play a lesser role and appeal for its protection against damage caused by the climate, or sanctify the motor car and sound off about the anti-social behaviour of the automobile corporations. The opinions of the public are weighed down with contradictions on such issues – a fact that is not really so very hard to explain. But this is enough to suggest the scale of the effort required to prepare a true citizens' debate.

In our attempt to combine global analysis with an introduction to political debate, we shall identify what really does seem to be a major aberration in our system of civilization: that is, the fact that those in charge use the accumulation of profit as almost the sole criterion for solving the problems of enormously complex societies. This will form the basis of our account of the economic, social, ecological and political impasses into which these societies have now been driven. In this sense, the book may be said to offer a critique of the overarching historical process of 'global marketization'.

But the aim of the book is also to show that it is still possible for our societies to extricate themselves from the impasses of marketization, and to promote a different kind of social progress. Finally, as a contribution to the sorely needed debate, it offers a number of markers towards alternative policies.

I should like to thank especially Maurice Bertrand, who encouraged me to take on the work of writing this book, as well as Jacques Généreux, whose rigorous criticisms enabled me to improve its construction. Thanks also to Jacques Grinevald, Marilu d'Onofrio, Andras November and Gilbert Rist, who read and criticized earlier versions either of particular chapters or of the whole work.

Christian Comeliau
Geneva, January 2000

CHAPTER I

INTRODUCTION

Let us take the six days of Genesis as an image and use it to picture what has actually happened over the past four billion years. One day roughly equals six hundred and sixty million years. Our planet was born on Monday at zero hour. During Monday, Tuesday and Wednesday a.m. the Earth was being formed. Life began at midday on Wednesday and developed in all its organic beauty over the next three days. Only on Saturday at four in the afternoon did the first reptiles appear. Five hours later at nine p.m., when the sequoias were rising from the ground, the large reptiles disappeared. Man only emerged at three minutes to midnight on Saturday evening. At a quarter of a second before midnight, Christ was born. At a fortieth of a second before midnight, the industrial revolution occurred.

Now it is midnight on Saturday, and we are still surrounded by people who think that what they have been doing for a fortieth of a second can go on indefinitely...

David Brower (quoted in René Passet, *L'Economie et le vivant*, p. 76)

A STATE OF DISARRAY[1]

Development, modernity, globalization, liberalization. Few epochs in human history have known as many upheavals as ours has known, especially in the course of the twentieth century, whose final decade, far from slackening the pace, brought a further major diffusion and acceleration of change in the shape of 'globalization'. Unless our eyes and ears are closed to the world around us, these transformations appear both as a source of collective satisfaction and pride, and as the object of gloom, unease and profound disarray.

Each of us has a more or less confused sense that fundamental changes have been taking place. To be sure, these bring with them potential or already actual progress: many improvements in material comfort, development of communications among people around the

I

world, constant retreat of famine and most major epidemics, raising of educational levels. But they also contain unusual and exceptionally grave threats to the future of our societies: local or more general wars, interethnic genocide, persistent stockpiling of weapons with a terrifying destructive power; extreme social tensions resulting from increased inequality, exclusion or marginalization (especially in the world of work); dangers of genetic manipulation and rapid degradation or even destruction of a large part of the natural environment.

Contrary to a naive view held for a number of years, these advances and threats are not shared between a dominant 'North' over here that has overcome most of its historic challenges and embarked on a road of unclouded progress, and a backward, dominated 'South' over there that is still temporarily sunk in poverty, political instability and generally outdated ways. The wake-up call for those who believed this has been loud and brutal. Poverty has certainly not disappeared from the South, but in the countries that used to think of themselves as 'developed' the economic apparatus has proved ever more clearly incapable of absorbing people in search of employment, and hence of justly distributing the fruits of growth. Instead, we have seen the unexpected return of acute forms of poverty in the midst of the world's richest societies. The ecological threats to the planet, though by no means fully appreciated, have become increasingly difficult to deny. The advanced countries have not yet satisfactorily integrated the dramatic economic and technological changes into their culture and their system of social relationships, with the result that the big city suburbs, in particular, have had their equilibrium seriously shaken. Finally, many political institutions appear less and less suited to the new realities; a number of countries liberated from totalitarianism (including some of the most powerful) are on the brink of anarchy, and localized but bloody wars have again broken out at the heart of Europe.

Strictly speaking, there is no longer a 'third world' – partly because the 'second world' of the Soviet bloc has collapsed, but above all because the countries of the South have themselves become profoundly diversified. There are now few elements really in common, and there is therefore little scope for united political action, between the 'newly industrialized countries' geared to exports and queuing up to join the OECD, the Arab world torn between modernism and fundamentalism, the increasingly impoverished countries of Africa, and the Indian and Chinese giants. The Asian crisis of 1997 cast doubt upon what were, until recently, considered the most promising development trajectories in the South. 'North–South relations' themselves, which structured international history for four decades in tandem with 'East–West relations' (or rather, in subordination to them), are undoubtedly a less and less important category for social analysis and political action in the context of *fin de siècle* globalization.

The unity of planet earth is at once tighter and looser than in the past. The challenges of life in society have become immeasurably more numerous and diverse, though also strangely similar from country to country in their key characteristics. Indisputable advances take place alongside extreme disarray, abject poverty and unprecedented tragedy. But among the false prophets, the unkept promises and the threats of irreparable catastrophe, the traditional references upon which societies and cultures used to fall back have grown dimmer and largely unavailing. Hence the apparent contradiction when the social changes of modernity seduce large areas of the planet, yet also cause profound distress. Of course, we keep wanting to improve our level of material comfort, to travel to more distant parts, to benefit from the latest medical advances. But at the same time, we wonder whether our children will have to face war or ecological disaster, whether they will be able to find work, whether city life will remain bearable, whether each of us will endure solitude, or even more starkly (for those who are not among the earth's privileged) whether we will still have enough to eat tomorrow.

In view of this sense of contradiction, anxiety and impotence before a situation that confronts thousands of millions as they go about their daily lives, it seems impossible simply to leave it at that, to give up any attempt at explanation and action, to close one's eyes in resignation. True, no one today can claim to provide a fully satisfactory interpretation of this gigantic challenge, still less an immediately workable solution to all the problems that it poses; but if we reject fatalistic passivity, we must make a start at identifying and clarifying the most crucial questions. This will bring us closer to an understanding of what is truly important in the changes taking place before our eyes (in their global dimension more than their local specificities, for the dominant growth model aims to be planetary in scope); it will also allow us to explore the basic elements of a response that are already available, or remain to be worked out.

A CONTRIBUTION TO ANALYSIS AND DEBATE

This book is intended not as a deep and thorough analysis, but only as a rough outline that will, I hope, encourage further reflection and synthesis. Steering clear of both amateurish simplicity and technocratic pseudo-certainty, it will seek to understand the nature of present trends, the logic (or lack of logic) underlying them, and the fundamental problems they raise. The main objective is to contribute to the debate in society at large, which is becoming ever more essential.

The reflections will be organized as follows. Chapter 2 aims to spell out the main facts that have given rise to the spreading sense of unease. Chapters 3 to 5 then suggest some initial hypotheses to guide our analysis of social change, some of whose characteristics (and contradictions) may be observed in varying degrees among the most diverse societies in the world, but which can nevertheless be tied up with a common 'development model' of what we shall here call 'modernity'. The main features of this model are the following: it is *historically contingent*, and therefore does not represent an unavoidable necessity; it confers exceptional importance upon *economic concerns*; it claims to be *expansionist*, and to be the dominant influence on the whole world. Here we should stress the rise of individualism and the growing pre-occupation with economics – the very two foundations, as Louis Dumont has argued,[2] of the 'economic ideology' or the ideology of modernity.

The essence of Part One is thus an attempt to show some of the most salient features of this dominance of economics, to identify its inner systemic logic. Chapter 4 defines what we might call the 'market or commodity relationship' that is at the heart of the economic and social organization of our world. Chapter 5 draws out the dynamic of needs and the thinking that claims to justify it, but then goes on to expose the inadequacy of this partial logic, and to consider the possible criteria of a more inclusive rationality.

Part Two consists in a closer study of some of the main problems resulting from the systemic logic identified in Part One: the absurdity of the requirement of indefinite growth, and the inevitable limits of this onward rush (Chapter 6); the various impasses that have led to an international demand for 'social development' – especially those resulting from sharper inequality (Chapter 7) and those threatening the future of work and employment (Chapter 8); and the worldwide deepening of systemic contradictions in the wake of globalization (Chapter 9). Finally, by way of transition to more directly political matters, Chapter 10 examines the uncertainties affecting the present role of public authorities.

Part Three is conceived as an introduction to the political debate. Chapter 11 spells out the reason for the debate, as well as its essential nature and requirements. Next, since modernity is ultimately based upon the system of values that it defends, Chapter 12 turns to a survey of the dominant values, and opposes to them what might be a different ethic, one built around a new conception of liberty, solidarity and responsibility. Finally – at a rather general level made necessary by the fact that more specific solutions can refer only to specific communities – Chapter 13 proposes some goals and priorities of alternative policies, as well as some of the instruments that might be used to achieve them.

ALIENATION AND FALSE PROMISES

Such is the approach I have in mind. But perhaps the general drift of the analysis, and even more the call towards the end of the book for a political debate, will be better understood if I outline straight away the main conclusions of the analysis, and the way in which they might serve as a starting point for debate.

The first conclusion is that the societies already formed (or now being formed) in accordance with the dominant model of modernity are marked by profound alienation, and this is why a radical ethical critique of their main features is required. It is an alienation through technology and through economics – or rather through a market form of economics that spreads its own distinctive values. It is an alienation made worse by the general pressure for imitation exerted by the dominant model – a phenomenon that is not peculiar to contemporary societies (one has only to read René Girard to be convinced of this[3]) yet intensively exploited by an economic system that certainly is peculiar to them.

Now, the defining feature of alienation is that it prevents us from being ourselves; it dissociates our goals, actions and modes of relating to society from the real world and its requirements for harmony and survival. This fundamental unreality is present everywhere in the accelerated evolution of our societies, which want everything at the same time, identify well-being with the possession of money and ever greater consumption of commodities (food, cars, luxury goods, drugs), and successfully confront the most extraordinary challenges (space conquest, information superhighways, genetic mutation, or certain sporting feats). For they are also societies which increasingly fail to satisfy certain of their vital needs: access for all to a decent standard of living, through a job or any other means; safe and peaceful relations among individuals, ethnic groups, nations or religions; the eradication of poverty, unacceptable inequalities and systematic exploitation of the weakest by the strongest; or a halt to the overconsumption of non-renewable resources which has been growing at a rate never before seen in history. These contrasts are part and parcel of the prevailing alienation – both because they hardly seem to trouble the 'culture of contentment',[4] and because they continue to exert a seductive power over the great underprivileged majority.

This leads to the second, even more pessimistic conclusion, which conflicts so sharply with the triumphalist talk of progress and development. It is that our system of 'modernity', for all its expansionist pretensions, *is neither generalizable nor viable in the long term.* This means that we will have to change the system ourselves, or else endure change without being able to master it.

On any estimate, it is intolerable hypocrisy on the part of those who are responsible for social progress and collective development to continue speaking and behaving 'as if' the dominant model from which a minority benefits so much today were not only viable – or 'sustainable', to use the current jargon – but capable of spreading to the four corners of the earth. But that is precisely what our whole system of economic and social relations, as well as our criteria for individual or collective promotion, implicitly assume. This assumption is powerfully supported, moreover, by the demand for expansion of the world economy itself, by the propaganda of the most influential media, and by what is called 'development aid'.

I argue that it is not only desirable but possible to escape this impasse, though the enterprise will be long, complex (because our societies have themselves grown complex) and extraordinarily demanding. It will be necessary to shake off the yoke of the absolute domination of economics, so that a debate about social goals can once again become possible. It is in this perspective that we can speak of a 'quest for meaning'. Ethical and philosophical reflection must play a major role here in preparing the options, as must economic analysis. But the debate will be essentially political, because it concerns the goals that society should set itself.

Contrary to any 'one-dimensional', Manichean opposition between the extremes of unrestrained liberalism and authoritarian centralism – both of which have been rendered defunct by the very complexity of contemporary societies – I would suggest that a number of different means and strategies might be employed for the achievement of these goals. They will have to give a central place to changes in the social rules of the game, and therefore to the creation of more suitable institutions. They will also require the support of political and social forces capable of asserting themselves against the most conservative interest groups.

In spite of the very general level that we are forced to adopt in analysing these questions, and therefore in spite of the sometimes abstract or even theoretical appearance of the argument, it should again be stressed that the political issues at stake are extremely concrete. Thus, the collective debate can and must proceed in highly practical terms — on condition that the social forces involved are sufficiently aware of what is at stake. The aim of this book is to contribute to such an awareness.

PART ONE

THE LOGIC OF MODERNITY

CHAPTER 2

THE FACTS OF CHANGE
AND UNCERTAINTY

It has become almost commonplace to underline the depth and diversity of the economic and social changes that took place in the second half of the twentieth century, in both the industrialized and the so-called developing countries. We shall not attempt here to tabulate these advances or the opposing tendencies that accompanied them, but shall simply mention some particularly significant figures relating to the accelerated progress and 'development' of recent decades. Attention should also be paid, however, to some of the negative aspects of these changes, which have long been passed over in silence, or regarded as inevitable secondary difficulties that will prove to be no more than temporary. Today these negative aspects seem to be approaching a critical threshold, and therefore appear to be major obstacles to progress which call into question the long-term viability, and even the desirability, of the new directions of change. The key question, then, is whether positive changes and negative changes are separable from each other, or whether they are two sides of a single tendency that no one controls any longer.

GLOBAL INDICATORS

The substantial economic and social progress of recent decades is an undeniable fact. Let us take some very general figures for the whole world (intentionally not for the poorest countries alone), starting from the conventional measure most widely used in relation to development, namely gross domestic product per capita or – what comes to much the same thing in most cases – income per inhabitant. Since 1960, according to the United Nations Development Programme report for

1997, average income per person (in 1987 US dollars) for all the developing countries rose from $330 in 1960 to $671 in 1980 and $832 in 1994; the corresponding figures for the industrial countries were $6,448, $11,562 and $14,473, and for the whole world $2,049, $3,205 and $3,403. In the space of thirty-five years, global per capita income thus increased by a factor of 2.5 in the developing countries, 2.2 in the industrial countries, and only 1.7 in the world as a whole, because of the sizeable gap (18 to 1) still separating average incomes in the South and the North.[1]

Although these growth tendencies are considerably higher than in previous eras, they may be regarded as fairly modest. The 1997 UNDP report, with its special focus on the elimination of poverty, nevertheless underlines the scale of the advances, especially if one looks beyond average income indicators.

> Few people realize the great advances already made. In the past 50 years poverty has fallen more than in the previous 500. And it has been reduced in some respects in almost all countries. The key indicators of human development have advanced strongly in the past few decades. Since 1960, in little more than a generation, child death rates in developing countries have been more than halved. Malnutrition rates have declined by almost a third. The proportion of children out of primary school has fallen from more than half to less than a quarter. And the share of rural families without access to safe water has fallen from nine-tenths to about a quarter. These advances are found in all regions of the world.[2]

Income growth in the industrialized countries, which was particularly rapid during the postwar 'golden age' between 1945 and 1975, has continued at a slower pace in the past twenty-five years. The variations have been greater in the developing countries, but today some regions are growing faster than the rich countries. Overall, of course, there is still a sizeable income gap between North and South; but what is less well known is that the disparities are smaller when development is measured not by per capita income but by such standard-of-living indicators as life expectancy at birth, infant mortality, educational level, access to drinking water, or food consumption levels. Thus, according to the UNDP, if the level in the industrialized countries is set at 100, then life expectancy in the developing countries rose from 67 in 1960 to 84 in 1994, adult literacy from 43 to 64, and daily per capita calorie intake from 72 to 82; the death rate for children under five remains more disturbing – only 21 to 29 on a similar scale in which the industrialized countries represent 100.[3]

The advances are not in doubt, then, and more economic figures could be used as yardsticks. Nevertheless, they do not account for all the observable changes; the evolution of human society can hardly be summed up in purely economic indicators. Without giving way to facile catastrophism, we may therefore also point to the emergence of negative aspects. These are hybrid in nature, and cannot always be precisely measured, but they have recently grown in importance to such an extent that they raise the question of a possible link with the positive indicators we have just mentioned. If such a link is established, the negative elements will appear no longer as a mere blip but as the other side of the coin of progress.[4]

After an examination of these negative aspects under four headings – living conditions, social cohesion, culture, and ecological balances – we shall consider whether it is still possible to believe in a long-term solution to the problems through a form of economic progress that simply maintains existing trends.

LIVING CONDITIONS

Let us begin with the material existence of individuals, in the most ordinary sense of the term. The major advances achieved throughout the world in less than half a century need to be related to the ever more powerful and sophisticated technological capacity of a productive system in which nothing seems to be out of reach any longer – from space exploration through instantaneous data communication to medical breakthroughs and genetic modification.

In this new world, however, poverty is far from having disappeared. The introduction to the 1997 UNDP report refers to poverty in developing countries, in a way that is hardly surprising; it simply tones down the enthusiasm stemming from naive and excessively compressed (or excessively biased) calculations – 'More than a quarter of the developing world's people still live in poverty', and 'about a third – 1.3 billion people – live on incomes of less than $1 a day.' But there is also poverty in the supposedly rich industrial countries of the OECD, where 'more than 100 million people live below the income poverty line, set at half the individual median income, [and] thirty-seven million are jobless'. 'Within these broad groups some people suffer more than others – particularly children, women and the aged.'[5]

We know also that, in at least part of the former Soviet bloc, the economic transition has brought with it a considerable deterioration in living conditions which most commentators simply assume to be no more than a 'transitional' phenomenon.

These data correspond to what each of us can observe every day, either directly or through the media. Similar indicators would express the worsening environmental and health conditions for large sections of the population, in poorly supplied rural areas but also in the big cities and sprawling suburbs, as well as the consequences of the huge waves of more or less forced migration. Hard to ignore – though less easy to measure – are the feelings of widespread frustration that inevitably arise in a context that sanctifies technological progress, rising income expectations and matching levels of consumption. We may identify (in the briefest outline) three characteristics common to all these situations: poverty, inequality and insecurity.

The definition of *poverty* has recently been the object of much controversy, which goes well beyond questions of terminology or statistical method. Let us for the moment adopt the UNDP perspective, without going into any further specifications that might be required. The consideration of human poverty, the UNDP report argues, 'focuses not just on poverty of income but ... on poverty as a denial of choices and opportunities for living a tolerable life'.[6]

The insufficiency of choices allowing a decent life is certainly the essence of the problem. This insufficiency is paradoxical, because technological progress achieves many results, and offers ever greater possibilities to an affluent minority. But the persistence – or re-emergence – of poverty means that for a large percentage of the world's population it is a serious problem to keep body and soul together, not to speak of enjoying a comfortable life. What international organizations call a situation of 'abject poverty' is not an invention of theirs, as anyone can verify for themselves. But just as much of a reality is the fear which has gripped people in the rich countries over the last couple of decades, concerning both the provision of their livelihood (witness, most spectacularly, the large-scale begging that has reappeared in most of the large Western cities) and the opportunities for their children to find a point of insertion into the allegedly so successful productive system. Perhaps the paradox should be taken even further. For the pressures of this system are such that the most privileged consumers see a kind of narrowing of their field of choice – either because considerations of social status force them to keep up with the neighbours, or because so-called corporate profit requirements come into play. But at least their right to go on living is not in question – which means that they remain privileged.

The difficulty of living, then, is not spread around equally; it is much more acute in certain regions, and among certain social classes or categories of individuals. *Inequality* remains present in the world, despite recent advances (in fact, it has never been absent). Although it has diminished in certain respects, it has considerably worsened in others: the gap between sub-Saharan Africa and the rest of the world, for example, or between rich and poor in the United States, between the middle classes and the majority of the rural population in India, and so on. The figures most often cited – by the UNDP and other pretty unimpeachable sources – all point towards the conclusion that an ever smaller section of the world's population holds an ever larger part of global income and resources.

Meanwhile, the big banks and corporations seem preoccupied with competitiveness, power struggles, 'mega-mergers' and turnover figures, rather than with their own function in society. As for the international organizations that tower over the world economy – the IMF in Russia, or the OECD and WTO in their more or less secret drive to put together a 'multilateral agreement on investments', or the same WTO in its unsuccessful attempt in Seattle in December 1999 to agree on a negotiating agenda on international trade – they often seem to veer only between impotence and knuckling under to the super-rich. The various states in the world, as we shall see, are asked to make do with a 'subordinate' role in relation to the market. In the end, then, it is hard to envisage that any countervailing power will emerge in the face of growing inequalities. The first difficulty, to which we shall have to return, lies in locating the origin of this process. Are inequalities simply the result of a general progression of wealth, which can never be homogeneous – and if so, how wide will the gaps become? Or does enrichment for some, perhaps even any improvement in their living conditions, necessarily entail impoverishment or a worse life for others?

On any hypothesis, one of the results of this poverty and inequality is an intensification of material and psychological *insecurity*. Many people do not know whether they will have enough to eat tomorrow, or even this evening; many people do not know whether they will keep their job for much longer; others feel less and less secure about their home, or their health, or their right to live in the country in which they were born, or even their capacity to go on living, or to remain in possession of the goods they cannot do without. As for collective safety in such matters as food supply, sanitation or energy – a problem one might have thought to have been definitively solved – new and legitimate concerns have recently been raised in connection with the activities of certain major economic players. Finally, we know from the UNDP report that at the end of 1997 there were officially almost 12 million refugees in the world.[7]

SOCIAL COHESION

The major changes in living conditions are those which lend themselves most readily to measurement, and this is why they have been cited as the main argument in glorifying the system. But these material changes have also transformed the structures that frame life in society: the family, both immediate and extended; affinity groups and social classes; links to public authorities, churches or private associations; relations between town and country, young and old, and so on. To be sure, such upheavals have not been passed over in recent social studies. But since they are less easily quantifiable, as well as bound up with value judgements, they have not been coherently or systematically integrated into analyses of the 'development process'. I shall not here propose a method by which this might be done, but I would like to touch upon a few of the main changes that seem to be directly linked to what has been noted above – particularly the consequences of uncertainty and insecurity, the degradation of what is rather mysteriously called 'the social fabric', and some elements of the framework and institutions of social life.

Uncertainty and *insecurity* are phenomena that relate primarily to living conditions, the means of subsistence, paid work, safety of the person and of individual possessions, civil order and international peace. We have already mentioned the symptoms of psychological anxiety and collective unease that are most frequently associated with these phenomena. But it is the viability and the organization of whole societies, not just the safety of individuals, which now appear to be under threat. The rising material prosperity of individuals and families was accompanied by various 'social' measures and regulations, whereby the community protected people's welfare in the event of age, illness or unemployment. But just now, when societies are becoming richer and more powerful, but also more unequal, there is talk of the inevitable drying up of public resources. In a move that is sometimes strangely muddled up with notions of decentralization, or even democracy, public authorities are denied the right to raise the necessary resources through personal and corporate taxation, and their responsibility for welfare protection looks set to be transferred to individuals (now supposed to be capable of protecting themselves) and private organizations. This is the reason for the growing insecurity at community level as a result of the growing 'flexibilization' of labour, the reduction of unemployment benefit, and the authorities' incapacity to eradicate certain types of crime (theft and corruption, sexual assaults, gun killings in the USA, criminalization of the economy in Russia, and so on).

The public weal is not the only issue at stake. For material advances have made economic concerns ever more decisive in social interchanges, and in most countries today economics is essentially market economics based upon competition and individual appropriation. As we shall see, at some length, its hold is so great that it tends to supplant all other forms of social 'regulation', particularly the traditional forms of solidarity represented by family, social group, occupation, age group or ethnicity. 'Lack of regulation' and 'destruction of the social fabric': these slightly abstract established formulas mean, in plainer language, that individuals are now alone. They are alone in the face of competition, profit motives, uncertainty, insecurity, and even brute force (when the authorities are unable to control it or, worse, use it themselves to defend private interests). Ultimately they are alone in the face of themselves, in so far as the erosion of family or neighbourhood, and the conversion of workmates into rivals, mean that they are no longer rooted in any natural networks of support. And they are left alone to search for an identity, in a fragmented and unfathomable world where the only refuge for community values is certain sporting occasions or pathetic televised games.

No one, we repeat, denies the reality of these upheavals. So are they the inevitable but temporary costs of a tendency whose generally positive character is in no doubt? Or are they irreversible phenomena, cumulative and linked to one another?

CULTURE

We may continue this enquiry by looking at some cultural aspects that are emerging under the influence of 'progress'. By 'culture', I mean here the reflection of societies about themselves, the value system they adopt within this perspective, and the meaning they claim to give to their own evolution. Can such a meaning be discerned in the actual evolution of things?

This question is obviously not one of those that can be answered in a few simplistic phrases. But it would seem that the accentuation of poverty, inequality and insecurity is inevitably worsening the 'state of disarray', to quote again the UNRISD formulation summing up the social effects of globalization. This expression is not only eloquent; it lights up the essence of the problem. People feel lost when they can no longer answer the questions relating to everyday life and social organization with which the invasion of economics presents them, and when 'the institutions of society have been not only disregarded, but treated as obstacles and shamelessly dismantled'.[8] So if there is no longer an identifiable framework for such answers, how can one still hope to discover a meaning?

This disarray in the face of economics is undoubtedly crucial to an understanding of numerous phenomena that everyone can see around them. The crisis of education, for example, both in the family and in school institutions, makes it difficult to give a meaning to an ever more fragmented educational system in the service of no one quite knows who or what (except the rather short-sighted imperatives of 'profitability'). Or take the yawning abyss of the leisure culture disseminated by television, the press and other major media (what Ignacio Ramonet calls 'mass culture', as distinct from 'scientific culture' or 'humanist culture'[9]); or the profound crisis of religion, which should be taken very seriously because it concerns not only antiquated forms of hierarchy, morality or liturgical practice, but the much deeper lack of a meaning that can be given, in our technological and economic world, to the fundamental human longing for transcendence. In fact, the modern economy may be precisely the most developed rejection of transcendence.

Lack of meaning, crisis of values, alienation, disarray: everyone feels more or less confusedly these new (or anyway, considerably aggravated) characteristics of our societies, with the collective and individual consequences they entail.

At the collective level, apart from a few slogans that are at most accepted with reservations, everyone agrees that it is extremely difficult today to interpret, summarize or formulate the main aspirations of a community, and to implement them in a programme of general and coherent change. There are no longer any political leaders audacious enough – or unrealistic enough – to formulate, and say they are carrying out, a grand 'design' or 'project' for society. A case in point would be the fate of what used to be known in France as the 'planning' institutions, which have now been unceremoniously 'laid off'. But more critically, communities have been breaking apart (in Rwanda, the former Yugoslavia, Russia, Indonesia and elsewhere), practising 'ethnic cleansing' on a mass scale or sliding into civil war.

At the individual level, the sense of disarray has been accentuated by the fact that this blurring of collective value systems and disappearance of most points of reference in the community have come on top of general feelings of uncertainty and job insecurity, in a context where isolation is more and more the recognized way of life for most people. We therefore see 'the rise of the irrational',[10] with such dramatic consequences as increased use of hard drugs, proliferation of sects, and higher rates of adolescent suicide. These phenomena can no longer be ignored. But are we ready to link them to a general interpretation of the evolution of economy and society?

THE ECOLOGICAL THREATS

In addition, there are other fears, not yet clearly formed in the minds of most people, which concern the balance of natural resources and, more generally, the ecosystems of planet earth.

Little by little, people are becoming aware of a feature that distinguishes our epoch from all others in history: the rapid consumption of the stock of non-renewable natural resources (or of resources which can be renewed only over a long period of time, or used only in conjunction with non-renewable resources). What I have in mind are energy sources and minerals, fertile soil and available forest, the diversity of living species, the ozone layer, and world water supplies (which, in the World Bank's view, could be one of the main sources of human conflict over the next century). Ramonet quite rightly speaks in this context of a 'Faustian threshold'.[11] Never has humanity occupied such an invasive position in the universe.

Since Bhopal and Chernobyl, we also know that certain threats linked to industrialization are not imaginary, even if they have been systematically denied or downplayed. We know that an accident in a chemicals factory can cause thousands of casualties: among people whose only mistake was to live in the vicinity, and whose right to compensation is not even recognized. We know that no frontier can protect a country from the passing of a radioactive cloud – indeed, we are told that the question now is not so much whether other Chernobyls could happen as when they will happen, and what new protective measures will be in place by then. We also know that nuclear energy use, and especially the radioactive waste resulting from it, pose a number of threats to the environment in the very long term – but that the completion of new nuclear projects was not held back until a satisfactory agreement on such matters had been reached. We know that even if the Cold War among the major powers has ended, the risks of nuclear (and biological) weapons proliferation, as well as the risks of terrorism, cannot be adequately contained by any protective system in place today – but also that the greatest hypocrisy prevails in this field of diplomacy. As the number of studies increases, and both the media and politicians are beginning to talk about such matters (albeit not with sufficient rigour), there is a growing suspicion that various harmful substances are unintentionally present in our lives, and that no one is even monitoring and controlling them, simply because they are the collective outcome of millions of seemingly innocent individual actions. The spread of industrial plant and means of transport is increasing carbon dioxide emissions, polluting the atmosphere and destroying the ozone layer; it threatens to induce global warming, and to change the climate in ways that would disastrously affect ocean levels and the amount of land available for farming.[12]

More than the social or cultural problems, these new ecological dangers are manifestly linked to forms of technological and economic change. And despite the offhand statements made by many of those responsible for such changes, it is difficult not to suspect that men have been playing the sorcerer's apprentice while leaving a number of central questions unresolved. These questions are neither secondary nor temporary, and they are adding to a sense of uncertainty about the long-term viability of the system that humanity has given itself. It is crucially important, therefore, to press on with the analysis and to consider the ways in which the various threats are 'systemically' connected with one another.

DEMOGRAPHY AND POLITICS

Lastly, we must consider some risks which had been thought of as things of the past, or treated in an often summary fashion. These are the risks bound up with population trends and their political consequences: not so much global overpopulation as more specific and localized (though still quite possibly major) phenomena. The recent massacres in Central Africa exceeded the most alarmist fears – can one talk about 'catastrophist exaggeration' when the catastrophes are already upon us? – and it is difficult to maintain that they had nothing to do with intolerable strains on the local demography. A distinction should be drawn here between risks linked to population *density* (which may seem too high for the resources of the area in question) and risks linked to the *rate of growth* of the population even at relatively low-density levels (a rate which may seem too high because of the extra investment and economic growth required, or because of the resulting proportions of the active and the inactive population). One does not have to be a global Malthusian to accept that population trends can still pose extremely difficult questions for development in certain regions and at certain periods, above all when they come on top of difficulties stemming from economic and geopolitical trends. Of course, such regional development problems also strengthen the migratory pressures (from Africa towards Europe, for example) which constantly worry the rich countries.

CONCLUSION: ALIENATION OR AN ECONOMIC RESPONSE?

The facts recalled in this chapter seem enough to suggest a startling picture of the changes that have taken place in recent decades. This picture reveals huge advances, but also raises disturbing questions about the long-term social, cultural, ecological and political 'sustainability' of the various observable shifts. It further arouses a sense of alienation − that is, a feeling that no one is in overall control of developments − and, more generally, serious doubts about the long-term viability of the system on which we find ourselves embarked.

We therefore need to make the questions rather more precise. What are the (necessary or contingent) links between the advances and the problems that present themselves? Should we simply consider that all progress demands sacrifices, and is it acceptable to put overall material advantages in the balance with social and ecological human costs? Is it possible to pursue a general strategy to raise income and production while avoiding the formidable obstacles described above?

A huge effort of enquiry and reflection will be necessary if we are to come up with at least a few answers. But one last point should be mentioned here, precisely because it offers a key for this enterprise of reflection. It is the fact that the system of 'modernity' itself seems to offer an overall response to the problems at issue, by referring to economics and 'economic rationality' as the dominant criterion. In this perspective, the above set of questions should all be given an affirmative, and therefore optimistic, answer: that the future of the system, and of social progress, will be assured in so far as the requirements of economic rationality are respected.

The difficulty, however, comes from the very specific (and historically quite exceptional) character of this economic rationality, which tends to consider that the advancement of the general interest will automatically follow from the free pursuit of diverse particular interests. It is this general hypothesis that must now be examined more closely.

CHAPTER 3

WHAT IS MODERNITY?

CHORUS: Did your offence perhaps go further than you have said?
PROMETHEUS: Yes: I caused men no longer to foresee their death.
CHORUS: What cure did you discover for their misery?
PROMETHEUS: I planted in their hearts blind hopefulness.
CHORUS: Your gift brought them great blessing.
PROMETHEUS: I did more than that: I gave them fire.

Aeschylus, Prometheus Bound, 247–52.[1]

The record drawn up in Chapter 2 may seem disheartening – not only because of its many negative or uncertain elements but also because its heterogeneity makes it difficult to find the lines of force. Let us now try to advance a little by examining the concept of 'modernity', which, together with the equally ambiguous concept of 'development', is often used to sum up our own epoch in comparison with those epochs that preceded it.

It is important to avoid a black-and-white analysis of a term that is so complex and so crucial for every one of us. Let us therefore begin by briefly recalling the main positive contributions of modernity, the product of the Enlightenment in opposition to the society of the *ancien régime*. We shall then see that present-day society and its model of development, whose main features were described in Chapter 2, may be interpreted as a quasi-pathological or deviant hypertrophy of some of the positive contributions of modernity.

THE MAIN CONTRIBUTIONS OF MODERNITY

Reason, the individual, social progress and new relations between the individual and the state: the picture is not complete, but in my view these four aspects sum up both the essence of 'modernity' and the source of the deviations that have brought about the present situation.

First, *reason* is universal in character, and is expressed in the capacity to explain and justify things that used to be thought of as dependent upon divine or human authority. Critical reason gave rise to the blossoming of education and the social sciences. It was applied to the history of individuals and societies (where it entailed an opening to knowledge of different societies), but above all to the present and future of individual behaviour and social organization. It therefore includes – in relation to modern societies – a capacity for self-criticism and self-questioning.

Since this universal critical reason is first of all the reason of *individuals*, their behaviour is profoundly changed as a result. The individual is now capable of separating off the secular from the religious, the realm of freedom from the realm of authority; he finds – or rather, considers – himself to be on an equal footing with other individuals, as well as with society and authority. Invested with a sense of responsibility and a capacity for initiative, the individual becomes a subject of choice free, in principle, from any influence of group or society, although by definition this involves at least potential competition with all other individuals. This situation of competition or rivalry, which reintroduces a reference to 'the other' and strengthens each person's imitative tendencies, leaves it uncertain whether the freedom of the individual is as great as he or she would like to think.

Beginning with the Enlightenment, this individual rationality is applied to the *goal of social progress*, a concept we have now integrated so deeply that we are scarcely capable of understanding its radical novelty in the eighteenth century. Social progress means that time is not necessarily repetitive, that tomorrow may be better than today. Presented in general terms as the march towards a better society, such progress involves a dual economic and political orientation. As a function of scientific and technological advances, it is expressed in economic progress. But since it reflects the quest for new types of relationship between individual, state and society, it also issues in new forms of political organization.

The advances of science and technology were at first driven largely by the state's quest for enhanced power (achieved through the efforts of military engineers and others). Economic progress was thus conceived first of all in collective terms, but the emergence of the individual as a subject of free and rational choice gradually steered it towards individual rather than collective goals. With regard to material resources, the conditions thus came into being for rational individual behaviour leading to the concept of *Homo œconomicus*, to utilitarianism and a formal theory of the market. The remarkable feature of the market was that it gave rise to a largely 'self-organized' society rather than to the building of a centralized organization. However, material resources could be freely allocated for individual goals only if certain institutional conditions were in place; the most important such condition, which underpinned the later domination of market economy, was private property and the associated power of individuals over things that grounded their freedom vis-à-vis other individuals. In the advent of industrial society, with its fantastic expansion of market economy spurred on by technological progress, the logic of private property led to an exclusive pursuit of individual interests, and hence to a disregard for the requirements of social justice and ecological sustainability.

As to the political organization inspired by these principles, it was supposed to establish new relations between the state (the public power responsible for collective actions with redefined goals) and the free individual endowed with critical reason. What resulted were societies based upon the concepts of human rights, equality before the law, citizenship and democracy, quite different from the birth, status and hierarchy integral to the *ancien régime* in that they combined notions of law and responsibility.

In sum, modernity appears in its principles as a harmonious blend of critical reason, individual liberty and responsibility, and a concern for social progress resting upon the advances of science and technology, industrialization and democracy. How could anyone complain about such a development?

This brief retrospect will, I hope, be enough to suggest that prudence is in order when it comes to a critical evaluation of modernity. Its main positive contributions are undeniably important, and have not been essentially called into question in contemporary societies – indeed, their ever wider recognition in principle (if not always their practical implementation) testifies to a seductive power which has lasted well beyond their original epoch. But why, in that case, should these contributions be associated with the mainly negative tendency presented in Chapter 2?

In a moment, we shall take another look at some of the main elements in the picture and try to locate them within an overall structural logic. But first it may be useful to summarize my interpretation of that overall logic. My working hypothesis is that the negative characteristics of present-day society and its model of development stem from the essential features of modernity – not as these exist in principle, but in a perverted, deviant form marked by what one might call a pathological imbalance between the initial components of modernity. This 'perversion' of the overall conception of modernity is displayed in:

* the centrality of individual and private values as against collective public values in human relations – even if this needs to be qualified in ways that we shall see;
* the systematic dominance of *economic* concerns over all other elements of social progress;
* the dominance of the logic of competition or rivalry over the logic of citizenship or solidarity, expressing economic concerns in an essentially market form and itself explaining partial rationality in terms of appropriable profit;
* the transformation of market economy into *capitalist* economy, mainly geared to the accumulation of profits on capital;
* the degradation of reason into the rationality of the accountant concerned with the accumulation of profit, as an effect of this capitalist market dominance.

Let us now take these elements in turn.

THE RISE OF INDIVIDUAL VALUES AND THE DOMINANCE OF ECONOMICS

Let us first note the spectacular rise of individual private values that today accompanies the global extension of 'modernity'. In contemporary lifestyles, the values of progress, comfort and all-round improvement of living standards, as well as the values of distinction and promotion within society, set up an opposition among individuals, and are intended to benefit particular individuals and the people immediately around them, much more than to strengthen social ties and mutual support. The first rule of life in modernity does seem to be 'everyone for themselves'. When a choice has to be made between these values, modernity most commonly sacrifices the old ties of kinship and social cohesion (family, ethnic group, village, social group, even nation) to the advancement of the individual's private life. It is individuals (or perhaps certain institutions acting in their name) who grow rich, acquire possessions, buy, exchange, save and accumulate; and if the distances or inequalities between them increase, this is but the inevitable consequence of a 'progress' which, though claiming to be general, cannot in the end benefit everyone at once.

In this context, public authorities still evidently address their discourse to the community as a whole, but the only meaning of this 'community' is that of a sum of individuals, as in Guizot's famous call: '*Enrichissez-vous!*' Did not Deng Xiaoping declare to the Chinese in 1978 that 'it is a glorious thing to become rich'?[2] And as for Margaret Thatcher (whose coming to power in Britain, shortly before Ronald Reagan in the United States, marked the ascendancy of neoliberalism in economic policy), her basic message was: 'I have never come across such a thing as society; all I know are individuals.' The political ideology of neoliberalism,[3] having thus achieved dominance, objected as much as possible to publicly held responsibilities and advocated a smaller role for the relevant institutions. It has been suggested that the welfare state itself accentuated this individualism, in so far as it enabled everyone to disencumber themselves from the other ties of mutual support.[4]

All is not quite so simple, of course, and community pressures often return in force. The first way they do this, as we have already noted, is through the spread of a gregarious mimetism of consumption, which is massively used by the advertising industry servicing the apparatus of commodity production. This new impetus to commodification helps to explain the grip of 'fashion' in so many areas of everyday life, the disproportionate role in our societies of what Georges Corm calls 'the king's fools',[5] and the growing exploitation of a system that raises certain individuals in entertainment and sport to the status of stars. Similarly, gregarious mimetism is at the root of the intellectual conformism of small closed 'elitist' circles – and also, perhaps, of the ideological consensus in France among intellectuals and politicians since the mid-1990s that has been described (with either a positive or a negative connotation, but usually without any analysis) as *la pensée unique*. Community feeling also wells up again – it is not always easy to know why – in such unexpected domains as television games and sporting activities; it has been claimed, no doubt with some exaggeration, that sport is the last bastion of nationalist sentiment.

Incomparably more dramatic manifestations of resurgent community, however, are the so-called 'identity crises' that can suddenly shake a whole region, ethnic group, religion or country, most often because a majority of its inhabitants or members have been unable or unwilling to integrate themselves along the officially recognized paths of modernity. To such collective crises, modernity tends to oppose the concept of 'human rights' – which is just as well. But it is also necessary to develop a better analysis of the ways in which modernity, property, competition and acquisitiveness have brought about situations where human rights are trampled underfoot. As everyone knows, crises of this type have taken an especially severe turn in recent years.

My second general point is that modernity is in essence primarily economic, in the sense that it places economic concerns at the centre of the system of values in society. What does this mean? What are these concerns, and how should they be characterized?

When it is presented as an individual and social appetite indissolubly bound up with 'human nature', consumption appears to be a primordial fact. Although this does not exclude more symbolic ambitions such as an improved social status, or even increased power, its most 'natural' objective is to secure greater material comfort through various goods and services: that is, through the consumption of commodities. The degree of material comfort is supposed to be proportionate to the total quantity consumed: more equals better. One of the first components of modernity, then, is the ideal of an indefinite quantitative increase in consumption.

But consumption presupposes production. Economic concerns therefore refer to productive activities – to their technical efficiency and their economy of means (especially time). In a civilization that continually draws inspiration from Prometheus, such concerns promote an ever more elaborate division of labour, and ever more sophisticated and 'efficient' productive technologies, as it is necessary all the time to produce more in order to consume more.

The goal of constantly raising production and consumption leads to the multiplication of various forms of exchange – the founders of classical economics even talk about a basic human propensity to exchange[6] – and therefore to general use of money. In this perspective, money is first of all an instrument of appropriation and, through the system of prices, a means of accounting in the exchange of commodity equivalents. But as trade grows more widespread and the effort to boost consumption and production constantly increases, money also becomes store of value, measure of profit and instrument of accumulation: accumulation of purchasing power, accumulation of profit, accumulation of savings as a precaution for the future, accumulation of power *tout court*. We shall see later that, as expressed in the central institutions of society (private property, wage labour, state servicing of the market, private enterprise and capital), the general commodification and pursuit of accumulation define a mode of economic and social organization that may be regarded as a pillar of modernity. This mode of organization is called capitalism.

The almost obsessional expansion of economic concerns also brings about their transformation. From a simple preoccupation with elementary or improved conditions of material subsistence, they become a systematic quest for efficiency and never-ending technological progress, as well as indefinite accumulation of profit for the purpose of enrichment and power. In recent years, thanks to an alliance of new information and finance technologies, this expansion has accentuated to an absurd degree the dissociation of finance from the real economy, so that speculation is now at the core of 'financial globalization' without necessarily resting upon an increase in real production.

With the advent of modernity, economics is no longer just one human activity 'embedded' in the other activities of society, to use Karl Polanyi's well-known expression referring to precapitalist societies;[7] it has become autonomous, developed a logic of its own, *imposed its domination over the organization of society as a whole.* The function of society itself thereby changes, as a general expansion of the economy seems to become its compulsory priority. And it is this expansion of modernity under the sway of economics that until a short time ago was known simply as 'development' – until, that is, a few sensible observers started adding various adjectives to clarify what kind of development they had in mind ('human', 'sustainable', 'social', and so on). But the basic paradigm of modernity – or, at least, the paradigm in its more recent, 'deviant' expression – has not been radically altered as a result.

Today, modernity appears as a source of numerous material blessings – that is clear. But the distribution of those blessings is far from equal, and – more important – their social costs are far from insignificant. Modernity tends to make of human society a collection of 'one-dimensional' beings,[8] whose concerns in life ultimately come down to material progress, profit and accumulation. It is a ground-level world, with no transcendence, no collective goals, no long-term perspective; its reasoning unfolds in purely individual and economistic terms.

LOUIS DUMONT ON THE ECONOMIC IDEOLOGY OF MODERNITY

Let us now place these two features – individualism and the dominance of economics – within the overall picture in which they are indissolubly linked, as the very essence of the 'economic ideology' underpinning modernity. It will be useful to recall here some of the salient points of Louis Dumont's synthesis of the 1970s, for they illuminate – perhaps better than any other – the social change we are trying to identify.[9] To

make the link with our present analysis, these points will be divided
into four groups.

1. Dumont defines ideology as the (more or less unified) 'set of social
representations', or 'the set of ideas and values common to a society'.
But unlike certain simplistic notions, which make it seem like a kind
of explicit reference map for one and all, the ideology of a society
remains largely implicit or unexpressed – hence the difficulty we have
in understanding ourselves, particularly in a period of 'paradigm crisis'
or 'revolution of values', and the importance of placing ourselves 'in
perspective'. The starting point for analysis and criticism of the 'economic ideology' must accordingly be the values upon which that ideology is based.

2. Dumont then draws a fundamental distinction between two types of
society.[10] On the one side are traditional or hierarchical societies, which
'value, in the first place, order: the conformity of every element to its
role in the society – in a word, the society as a whole'. Such societies
he calls 'holistic'. On the other side are egalitarian or 'individualistic'
societies, which 'value, in the first place, the individual human being'.
(We shall have to return to the paradox of this egalitarianism in principle in a world that is more and more inegalitarian in reality.)

'In the holistic type,' Dumont argues, 'the requirements of men as
such are ignored or subordinated; just as are the requirements of society
in the individualistic type.' Individualistic societies, with our own type
in the front rank, emphasize both equality and liberty, but the convergence of these two values is not guaranteed. However, it is above all
disparities in the relationship between wealth and power, and therefore
between economics and politics, which have the most profound
consequences.

The wealth of traditional societies is most often real estate, and power
is inherently linked to this form. Such societies are thus mainly concerned with *relations between people*. Modern societies, by contrast, are
born as formerly disdained movable wealth gradually spreads and becomes an independent source of power; then relations between people
yield first place to *relations between people and things*. Economics becomes autonomous from politics, 'embedding' itself in the relations of
society as a whole. (At this point the analysis joins that of Polanyi
mentioned above.)

3. Dumont considers the difficulty of defining this new economics in
a way that clearly distinguishes his approach from more traditional ones;

he mentions, in particular, the contrast between the 'formal viewpoint' largely accepted today, which focuses upon the different possible uses of scarce resources, and a more universal, 'substantive' approach which looks to 'the ways and means of the subsistence of men'.[11] What is certain, however, is that this newly autonomous economics is of a piece with individualism; the conception of the individual as the central player in production gives rise to the fundamental idea of mutually advantageous exchange. Individualism and the dominance of economics are confirmed as the two inseparable foundations of the ideology of modernity.

4. Utilitarianism, freed from traditional morality, becomes itself an ethic; for generalized exchange allows a spontaneous harmony of interests to take shape through the market. This is a traditional assertion of liberalism, but Dumont draws from it a number of implications that I shall oppose in a later section. It was the autonomy of economics, he argues, which made it possible to break hierarchical power and bonds of dependence between people; it is therefore crucially important to safeguard this principle of autonomy. Countries which tried to put an end to it (he mentions 'the authoritarian socialist countries', apparently including the Nazi regime) and to place the economy 'in the service of political and social goals' brought this about 'through oppression and in a spirit of contempt for the Individual'. Dumont therefore rejects any suggestion that 'the time has come to demote economics to a means toward the real (social) human ends'.[12]

Dumont's synthesis perfectly brings out the historical and ideological foundations of the present debate, throwing fresh light on it and on the questions that it poses for the future. Are we living at 'the end of history'? Are we forever confined within this historical legacy? If alternative solutions could be envisaged in previous epochs, can they still be envisaged today? Are the economy and society of modernity, as 'one-dimensional thought' claims, the only ones that can be practically contemplated for the future that lies ahead of us?

CAPITALISM AND MARKET ECONOMY

But before looking more closely at the nature and consequences of the market relationship at the core of modernity, we should remind ourselves that the framework for its expansion has been what is known as capitalism.

We cannot here undertake to describe the historical emergence and more recent development of the capitalist system, nor to set out in detail its founding principles at the level of economic theory. But we should at least point out that the new social features designated by the generic term 'modernity' – individualism and a concern mainly with economics – are also those which characterize 'globalization'. This latter term, which has been the height of fashion for several years, denotes a tendency for modernity to become general within all areas of human activity and all countries on earth. But in the end, it evokes no more than a quickening of the movement of exchange and accumulation that is peculiar to capitalism.

Capitalism itself may be understood as the most thorough institutional expression of modernity. It organizes the dominance of economic concerns within a Promethean productivist, and therefore expansionist, system, but at the same time it grounds this expansionism upon a generalization of the market relation and the indefinite accumulation of profit that it makes possible. The institutions of capitalism are built around a fundamental logic that unites: private property; private enterprise combining factors of production (essentially capital and labour – differentially remunerated as wage labour, interest rates and dividends – but also information); a generalized market; and a state based upon the rule of law, whose job it is to enforce the rules of the game in ultimate subordination to the smooth functioning of the market.

Since the market and the accumulation of profit have nothing to do with national frontiers, globalization merely accelerates the expansion of this capitalist logic to the whole world; one might even speak of the simple updating of a universal potentiality inherent within the capitalist system.[13] It should come as no surprise, then, that this latest stage of capitalism exhibits, with a few adjustments, the same rules and the same institutions as before: 'globalized' or transnational corporations, commercial and financial markets playing the role of supreme regulators, international public organizations in the service of these markets and promoting their expansion.

Capitalism is certainly not the only, nor the first, type of social organization to employ market mechanisms. *What is radically new is its claiming of the market as the sole foundation of its philosophy and organization, and the sole criterion of its further development, so that a cumulative process is unleashed which it is less and less able to control.* I take the liberty of using italics to underline that the market becomes the *sole* criterion for the organization of the economy, because this is the key point of the interpretation proposed in this book.

Before we turn to an account of the market – or, to be more precise, of the market relation – we should finish this chapter by reviewing the three characteristics of capitalism that make it the expression of the model of modernity.

- The aim that capitalism sets itself as the dominant model is indefinite quantitative growth of consumption and production, but this is subordinated to indefinite accumulation of profit through the instrument of money and, more broadly, capital. It is enough that there should be growth in the opportunities for profit, which may be expressed according to circumstances in a number of different watchwords (maximization of turnover, of 'cash flow', of market share, or of external investment and takeovers), or be geared to financial speculation rather than growth of physical output. In any event, these themes can all be linked with the quest for indefinite accumulation of power, in the forms best suited to the requirements of the existing system.

- Capitalism, for the same reason, is expressed in a tendency to the maximization of exchange and, in particular, towards general marketization of the values exchanged. This extends to all possible domains, including those that are resistant in principle to the general process of marketization (labour being the most noteworthy example). It remains to be seen whether this marketization corresponds to the quest for use values, and therefore to real human needs.

- Lastly, capitalism acquires and adapts all the institutions necessary to the logic described in the preceding two points: legal institutions (private property, contracts, wage relations, etc.), freedom of enterprise, a stock exchange, state regulation and protection, multilateral organizations, and so on.

Capitalist globalization, through its ambition to generalize modernity, certainly does accentuate the risks of deviation mentioned in the Introduction. To understand this better, we must now examine more carefully the characteristics of the market relation and the consequences of its generalization.

CHAPTER 4

THE MARKET AND THE MARKET RELATION

[T]he faith upon which our economic civilization reposes, the faith that riches are not a means but an end, implies that all economic activity is equally estimable, whether it is subordinated to a social purpose or not.

R.H. Tawney, *The Acquisitive Society*, p. 33.

If we criticize economic theory, it is not because it fails to account perfectly for the social reality, but because it follows too closely the forms of this insane world.

Paul Dumouchel and Jean-Pierre Dupuy,
L'Enfer des choses, p. 11.

IDENTIFYING A LOGIC AND ITS DISTORTIONS

If the market relation is the core of modernity, and of the social system that it globalizes within the framework of capitalism, we need to understand its logic as rigorously as possible. What is distinctive about the market relation within economics more generally, if the latter is defined as *a set of modes of conduct designed to maximize (for a set of human beings) the satisfaction of various needs requiring the use of scarce resources?*

The answer to this question may be summed up in a few keywords, each of which designates a basic element in the market relation.

1. The first, and no doubt the most fundamental, is private appropriation of the goods, services or means of payment that are exchanged. The market relation appears as an exchange of 'exclusive' rights of access to resources (the term 'exclusive' having a less innocent resonance today than it seemed to have in the past). The possibility of exclusion implies that the goods and services in question can be divided up – economists

sometimes speak of the divisibility of the exchanged 'utilities' – but also that they can be quantitatively evaluated according to general and 'anonymous' criteria (that is, criteria that lack any reference to individuals or a particular social group).

2. The criteria for exchange to take place are *solvent demand* or purchasing power on the buyer's side (the market takes no account of any need unless it is accompanied by a corresponding ability to buy) and *profit maximization* on the seller's side, so long as these two positions pulling in different directions can be reconciled through a generally accepted system of prices. The market furnishes this system of prices as an anonymous product of the relationship between *all* demanders and *all* suppliers for *all* the goods exchanged, and therefore capable of being quantitatively evaluated. Let us underline, in passing, the paradox contained in this triple 'all': namely, the theoretical principle that the market functions perfectly only if it can be generalized. The tendency to generalization is all the more likely to prevail in that the market thereby asserts the particular interests of its main protagonists over and above a highly problematic 'general interest'.

We may also note that in a generalized market (that is, a market involving the total sum of products exchanged) a distinction between use value and exchange value is no longer necessary or, indeed, possible. I buy something only if its market price (that is, its exchange value) does not exceed the value that I myself attribute to it; and conversely, I sell something only if its market price at least equals the value that I attribute to it; but exchange is always possible for all the goods and all the services. Exchange is therefore king, and to be part of the generalized exchange is the only way that something can respond to needs in their infinite diversity. This exchange-king claims to enshrine consumer sovereignty (or at least, the sovereignty of the solvent individual consumer), since it makes the quest for profit coincide with the expression of needs.

3. The first two characteristics produce a basic competitiveness among all the players on the scene – or, to put it more plainly, a general rivalry among individual units rather than solidarity vis-à-vis the needs of individuals and groups within a community. In other words, when a market is generalized, it tends to substitute itself for all other social ties, and even to destroy any that might remain. Economists speak of 'the separability of individual preference functions in a market of pure and perfect competition'; or, more colloquially, one might simply say that

individual players reason only as autonomous individuals, never according to a link with a group.

4. Now, the market does in fact display a tendency to generalization, for two reasons that have already been stressed: a logical reason (the market and its system of prices function perfectly only if they can be generalized) and a historical reason (the emergence of profit-seeking capitalism favoured the generalization of the market by giving it an appropriate institutional environment). This environment includes, most notably, the safeguarding of private property and of contracts. But it also organizes the systematic promotion of purely individual rights in the face of any threat of collective encroachment; it is a set of inducements offered to private interests rather than to collective or public interests.

When market mechanisms become generalized, however, so too does the *logic* of the market, with all the consequences we have described. Capitalist modernity, centred as it is upon such a generalization, creates a cumulative and self-sustaining extension of the market domain, and hence of indefinite growth, which concerns at once the consumption, production and exchange of commodities and, above all, the accumulation of the means of profit. The growth imperative is thus an intrinsic part of the capitalist market economy.

These brief indications will suffice to convey the gist of what I want to say here. First, market economy is one type of economic organization among others, but it is particularly well suited to relations among individual interests when these are both in rivalry with one another and chiefly concerned with material advances that can be expressed in individual terms. Second, market economy sustains and reinforces its own mechanisms, converting them into instruments of a blind and never-ending race for quantitative growth; the engine of this race is the accumulation of profit, its chief tool is money. Third, and most important of all, market economy contains within it a powerful urge to penetrate all territories and domains of human activity and social relations; so long as it is strengthened and even sanctified by institutions (as it is in capitalism), it displays a systematic tendency to dominate the whole organization of society – its values, rules and conduct – all over the world.

We can now more fully grasp that the degradation of our social system is linked with the structural characteristics of capitalism, which claims the market as the *sole* basis of its philosophy and organization, as well as the *sole* criterion for its actions and evolution.

This dominance of market economy, which gives the present stage of global evolution its distinctive features, explains at least the most serious of the threats weighing upon the organization of society. But before we come to these threats, we must identify some negative aspects of the basic logic that has just been described.

MAJOR DEFICIENCIES

1. The simplest expositions of capitalist doctrine deny that there is an opposition between 'economy based on profit' and 'economy based on needs'. As Adam Smith famously put it: 'It is not from the benevolence of the butcher, the brewer, or the baker, that we expect our dinner, but from their regard to their own interest.'[1] Needs are satisfied for the simple reason that this makes a profit for the person who satisfies them. But is this always the case?

The first point to be made is that, as these theorists admit, the 'optimization' promised by the perfectly competitive market assumes a set of conditions so restrictive that they are very rarely met – conditions such as a large number of players, none powerful enough alone to influence the choice of others; the divisibility of goods and services so that they can be appropriated in the desired proportions; the absence of increasing returns, perfect information about needs, the means to satisfy both those needs and market conditions, and so on. In any event, the ostensible 'optimum' is only relative in nature, a 'Pareto optimum',[2] because it is defined by reference to the initial distribution of purchasing power. The actual outcome is therefore likely to be less seductive than the one foreseen by theory – especially when the theory turns into ideology, as it seems to do in the case of 'neoliberalism'.

The 'consumer sovereignty' so proudly acclaimed by neoliberal doctrine is, in the end, only the sovereignty of the individual who can afford to buy the commodities in question at the market price. And even that sovereignty is limited on all sides, as the producer – whose motives have more to do with profit than with philanthropy – continually attempts to set constraints, and to mould the customer's choice through advertising and other devices. The money criterion therefore always prevails over the objective urgency or social legitimacy of needs – not through some deviation but as part of the system itself. Or rather: individual, and hence also social, priorities have no other way of expressing themselves than through the power to purchase commodities on the market.

Unless counteraction is deliberately taken at the level of the community, the main deficiency of such a model is its disregard not only for *non-solvent needs*, however urgent they may be even for human survival (the starving person has no right to a single crust of bread unless he or she pays the right price), but more widely for *collective needs* in general: that is, it takes no account of needs whose satisfaction does not pass through the private appropriation of certain goods and services (a highway will never be funded by an individual, because even a toll charge could never fully 'recoup the costs' of the investment). We might also add most of the needs which stretch out over a long period of time: the conservation of natural resources and ecological balances, for example, as well as education, public health, or basic scientific research. The reason is that, in the long term, the price system is incapable of providing the synthetic indicators that it offers in the short term, since the demand and supply cannot then be clearly expressed. Who, for example, is willing to sacrifice an individual possession, enjoyment or profit on the questionable grounds that such an act would protect the ozone layer?

This disregard for collective needs in the pure market model is largely admitted in economic theory and practice. Some kind of provision is always made for these needs, if only because it is essential to keep up a minimum of collective services – beginning with the maintenance of public order, currency regulation and basic infrastructure – for the functioning of any production or exchange. All economies existing today are therefore 'mixed', in the sense that they combine market mechanisms with various types of collective intervention. The problem persists and worsens, however, when society enlarges to the maximum the realm of the market and the proportion of non-solvent or collective needs for which it does not take responsibility. This is precisely what is happening today with the extension of capitalist modernity in a framework of neoliberal globalization – especially as other factors are increasing the pressure in the same direction.

2. Second, the market logic within a capitalist framework is weakened by a fundamental contradiction that is less and less successfully concealed. For this logic rests upon a dual assertion: on the one hand, it claims to solve, in the most rigorous possible manner, the basic economic problem of the tension between needs and scarce resources; on the other hand, it does not stop at stating (as all the elementary manuals claim) that 'needs are satiable yet ceaselessly renewed', but further maintains that human needs are by definition limitless – or more, that

because of its capitalist link with the accumulation of profit, the market logic imperiously requires needs to be limitless, and will do everything to ensure that they remain so. This contradiction may seem surprising to the uninitiated; it deserves a few moments' consideration.

Where does the scarcity come from? With a continuing appearance of good faith, the standard economic reasoning considers that it comes only from insufficiency of the means which, at any given moment and more generally throughout human evolution, are given us by nature and by man's technological capacity to transform it. This insufficiency, we are told, arises because the number of people on earth is ever growing, their needs are satiable but numerous and constantly reborn, their longing for material progress is an inescapable fact (whatever the legitimacy or urgency of each of the needs they express), and this longing is further accentuated by the imitative 'demonstration effect' of other people's behaviour. What can anyone do to change all this?

But here, a critical analysis of capitalist modernity casts the dynamic in a different light. First of all, it situates the question of scarcity within a much wider, 'eco-systemic' perspective in which resources are not infinite, and the general process of 'entropy' slowly but surely reduces the quantities of energy available for human use. Entropy, in other words, increases long-term global scarcity. We shall return to this point.

There are graver aspects. In the face of global scarcity, the economic reasoning inherent within capitalist modernity actually asserts that human needs have no limit — a move which sharply distinguishes such modernity from most other forms of economic organization observable, for example, in traditional societies. (Some iconoclastic anthropologists have even shown that a number of primitive societies were veritable 'societies of abundance'.[3]) However, the assertion that human needs are limitless does not flow from a purely theoretical position; it corresponds to an inner logical necessity. Since modernity is organized around indefinite growth of consumption and production, it rests upon a mechanism of cumulative creation of needs, and is thus in a position of systemic dependence upon growth. This dependence is indeed accentuated by what drives the system: the quest for profit and the indefinite accumulation of profit. We shall return to this at some length in Chapter 6.

But if modernity is so profoundly dependent upon growth, the standard economic perspective needs to be reversed: it is not the satisfaction of needs which is held back by an externally imposed scarcity of means, but scarcity itself which is the unavoidable result of a mode of human organization geared to limitless growth of needs (a growth ultimately explained and justified by the limitless growth of profit that it permits).

Some twenty years ago, Jean-Pierre Dupuy highlighted this paradox by drawing on the thought of René Girard and Ivan Illich. The genius of Illich, he argued, was 'to have understood that, once certain bounds are passed, phenomena can become inverted and men's efforts can produce the *opposite* of what they intend'.[4] But if this is correct, the implications must no longer be underestimated. We can speak of a veritable 'return of the tragic',[5] such that modernity is doomed because limitless rivalry and indefinite growth are the source of never-ending scarcity. In an inevitably limited world, history will have to end badly – unless we agree to reintroduce various forms of mutual support and general interest transcending the rivalry of particular interests.

3. The third systemic consequence of market mechanisms, linked with erosion of the distinction between exchange value and use value, is the confusion or even inversion of priorities that such erosion causes between the means and the ends of economic activity. The substitution of means for ends is 'the essential evil of mankind', wrote Simone Weil.[6]

The most spectacular, and certainly the most topical, example of this confusion is the emergence of the concept of 'human resources'. In the 1940s Karl Polanyi was already denouncing the commodification of labour.[7] Market mechanisms, and especially the 'rational' calculation of profit, were in principle no more than an instrument in the service of people and society. But the generalization of the market was sanctifying the accumulation of profit, transforming it into an end in itself for the agents dominating the market, and thus reducing human beings to 'resources' serving that sanctification. Education, health, security, even democracy – the problem of employment is so central that we shall have to return to it at length – were no longer objectives in themselves, but instruments serving growth and the profits it generated; their pursuit was subordinated to the usefulness they might or might not have for growth.

The confusion between ends and means has spread to many different domains. Here we shall mention only a few particularly striking and topical instances: the simplistic way in which multilateral financial organizations conflate the development of a national economy and its international competitiveness and export performance; the absolute priority that countries which can afford it give to balanced budgets, price stability and a strong currency, even to the detriment of the essential needs of certain social groups; the confusion that various social movements have recently shown between public services and the interests of wage-earners working in them; the preferential allocation of public resources to the maintenance of certain banking institutions, at a time when they have demonstrated their inefficiency even in purely market terms. More generally, the sanctification of growth – or, to be more precise, of hope in the return of growth – has appeared in political discourse of every provenance, both as an end in itself equated with human well-being, and as the only means of restoring full employment.

In the end, the assertion that human needs are limitless – an assertion which leads to the demand for indefinitely rising production for profit – is at the heart of an economic contradiction. This consists in the fact that limitless needs and growth are *the supreme form of the inversion of ends and means, peculiar to a profit-oriented economy that takes itself for an economy oriented to needs.*

4. A fourth set of difficulties arise from what at first seems a precious quality of market economy: its apparently 'spontaneous' or unorganized character, which has even led some of its devotees to assert that the market is the 'natural' form of economic and social relations, and to regard any intervention by an external authority as an inherently suspect 'distortion' of this 'natural' economic order.

This much-touted 'spontaneity' is largely an exaggeration, since the reality of actually existing market economies is one of considerable complexity. From this viewpoint, the neoliberal acceleration of modernity presents an astonishing paradox. Since it disregards non-solvent or collective needs, its logic is what lies behind the multiplication of economic, social and ecological problems. By virtue of its fundamental individualism, however, the same logic increases the obstacles to the creation or smooth functioning of institutions that could answer these collective problems – first and foremost, the public authorities themselves, and the rules of public order that they lay down. Manifest though some of these defects are, the market claims to be self-regulating, and rejects as illegitimate any attempt to regulate it from outside. In other words, the market's claim to generalization means that it is in need of institutions and rules – but it pretends to be ignorant of this.

What, then, are these rules for the functioning of the market which are all the more essential as it becomes more general? Rules are certainly necessary for the maintenance of public order and fair dealing in market exchanges, as are rules that specify the institutional grounding of the market (above all, private property and contract law) or control the emission and circulation of the currency. More broadly, there must be rules to define the rights and duties of individuals vis-à-vis the community, and in particular to specify the modes of distribution of the surplus and the remuneration of the different factors of production: who owns capital, how wages are fixed, what share belongs to the company, what share should rightfully go to the community in the form of compulsory charges. Other rules set limits on the realm of profitability, and therefore on the realm of the commodity. Under what conditions can labour be regarded as a commodity? Can heavy weapons, hard drugs, human beings or human organs be freely traded as commodities, with profit as the only criterion? Can the commodity world alone decide on people's reputation, their private life, their personal relations, their right to a decent material existence?

When the market rulers deny public officials the right to interfere in such matters, citing the principles of free trade and free enterprise, the demand for regulation of all these problems does not remain unanswered for long. But the answer is given by the private players who dominate the market, instead of being framed in the public interest. In fact, in the very conception of the market, the public interest exists only as the sum of solvent particular interests, and partisans of 'optimization' through the market (are they aware of this word's pretensions?) frequently omit to point out that the negotiating powers at the disposal of these particular interests are far from equal. Again we see how unrealistic are the hypotheses of pure and perfect competition... The remuneration of factors of production is an especially striking illustration, should one be needed, of the bias that market relationships of force introduce into the rules of the game. Whether at the level of nations or at the level of firms, the requirements of austerity are systematically deflected from capital towards labour, and we know today that share values never look better than when companies are laying workers off.

The sphere of market economy tends to encroach more and more upon that of the collective or public economy, on the (false) grounds that it is more 'natural' and does not require organization. The constant temptation for the market to govern the totality of social relations thus appears to be a fundamental phenomenon with numerous consequences. We have just noted the absence of regulation, or the privatization of modes of regulation, and we could continue in the same vein by discussing the privatization of all the prerogatives of the public authorities, as well as the so-called phenomena of corruption, which are very similar in nature.

More fundamentally, it is the central place of money as exchange value and instrument of private appropriation which explains the constant sliding of the economy in general towards market relations. It is evidently in these terms that we can analyse the recent globalization of finance, and the dissociation it enshrines between the real economy and the financial sphere.

CHAPTER 5

IN SEARCH OF AN OVERALL
ECONOMIC RATIONALITY

[E]ven if we accept the virtues of the competitive market ('the first computer available to men', according to Oskar Lange), we must at least point
out that the market was but an imperfect link between production and
consumption, if only because to some degree it remained incomplete. Let
me stress the word: *incomplete*. Actually, I believe in the virtues and the
importance of a market economy, but I do not think of this economy as
excluding all other forms.

The preserve of the few, capitalism is unthinkable without society's active
complicity.

Fernand Braudel, *Afterthoughts on Material Civilization
and Capitalism*, pp. 44, 63.

THE INADEQUACY OF A PARTIAL LOGIC

The account of the deficiencies of a logic of modernity based upon
generalization of the market results in a radical questioning of that
logic, for it highlights the partial character of a model that claims to be
total.[1]

The model is partial because it takes economics as the central − if
not the only − concern of human societies, and because it systematically prioritizes market economy among all other forms. It thereby
promotes mainly individualist and materialist values, and fails to recognize any kind of transcendence; it does not necessarily disregard other
values, but it always subordinates them to economic values. Various
authors have drawn on this insight to describe Mafia violence, for
example, as a predictable result of capitalism.[2] The general interest that
this model claims to promote has no content other than a sum of
particular interests where the market (that is, solvent demand) is arbi-

44

ter; its basic logic disregards collective or non-solvent needs unless their minimal satisfaction somehow affects the smooth functioning of the market itself, but most often it does not even allow them to be expressed. It recognizes only very few public regulations, generally replacing them with the most powerful market players as the ultimate court of decision.

More broadly, wherever market rationality acquires dominance, it transforms *social relations in their entirety*. Resting as it does upon private appropriation and competition, it entails individualist rivalry far more than mutual support as the basis for relations among the members of a society. It thus has a destructive impact upon the 'social fabric' itself. These points are by now so familiar as to be a little trite, but they correspond to quite definite realities that it would be wrong to ignore. In particular, they explain the growing significance of loneliness in daily life and the intensification of feelings of uncertainty or anxiety – in a social environment where the causes of insecurity and isolation keep multiplying.

The characteristics we have just described flow from the logic of the market. This logic cannot, of course, simply be rejected out of hand; historical experience cannot be ignored, and today there is a virtual consensus that market mechanisms are the best – or, anyway, the least bad – means to solve a large number of practical economic problems. I will therefore again make clear the scope of my critique. The difficulty stems not from the market as such, but from its almost *exclusive* use to solve the great majority of economic and social problems.

This is the heart of the matter. It may be objected that all systems of human organization are imperfect – so why keep harping on about this one, especially if everyone admits that it has a number of irreplaceable qualities? The reason is that the market model, in its neoliberal application, stakes out a truly *totalitarian* claim to invasive generalization whose results can be seen in the current pressures for globalization, and whose dangers become apparent in light of the overall analysis attempted in Chapters 3 and 4. For what has been shown is that modernity permitted and encouraged the passage from a model for the organization of certain definite economic relations to a model for the organization of society; from the partial mechanisms of market economy to a *market society* that aims to spread those mechanisms to all areas of life.

There remains, of course, the much more specific question of how all this happened. What explanation lies conveniently sheltered behind these logical principles? Since human history manifestly does not unfold in obedience to any logic or theory, are such principles and requirements anything other than general pretexts to justify particular ambitions?

There is probably no overall answer to this question – at best we can perhaps suggest elements of one. There is a fairly widespread tendency among human beings to give short-term preference to their own or their family's interests over those of a larger, and therefore more anonymous, community. There is also a temptation (obviously strengthened by the catastrophic Soviet experience) to adopt the easy solution of a supposedly natural and spontaneous mechanism, rather than the constraints of authoritarian collective organization. But these elements do not add up to a sufficient explanation; we still lack distance, and are still not familiar enough with the history.

Nevertheless, these difficulties do not release us from the task of facing up to the historical situation that they concern. If it is true that the *overall* organization of the societies of neoliberal capitalist modernity is entirely subordinate to the *partial* economic logic of the market, then political debate about the general organization of society – which was presented as desirable in the Introduction to this book – appears to be more necessary then ever. The contribution that economic reflection can make to this debate is now clearer: it can show the possibility of a general or overall economic rationality whose rules go beyond the realm of market economics.

THE REQUIREMENT OF
AN OVERALL RATIONALITY

In this section, we shall first recall what the search for a general economic rationality implies about the relationship between needs and scarcity. Next we shall show that the market expression of the requirements of such a rationality is only one particular variant, limited especially by its institutional assumptions, and that it is necessary to find a more general expression. The requirement of solvency, for example, does not have to be individual; nor does that of efficiency have to be fused with profitability. The conclusion will be that a broader, 'mixed' type of economic organization is necessary, especially with regard to the expression of needs and the conditions (private or public) of the response that can be given to them.

Let us keep our initial propositions as simple as possible, without losing ourselves in the many disputes over terminology. The tension between needs and scarcity, within a community whose members are engaged in exchange, is at the core of economic theory. The satisfaction of needs is the end in view, but this runs up against the (real or artificial) scarcity of the available resources, whose different possible uses entail that the various needs are in competition with one another. Needs satisfaction therefore requires the players – that is, members of the community with decision-making powers – to make certain allocation choices. Let us accept that the problem of economics relates in principle to this tension between needs and resources, and neither to the nature of human needs (which are extremely diverse, and have been classified in many different ways, Maslow's being one of the most notable) nor to their origin (physiological, cultural, mimetic or other). Let us also accept – a key point for defining the purpose of this chapter – that the choice of goals to be satisfied results from a value judgement on the part of those who make the decision, not from economic rationality in itself.

The rationality requirement is obviously linked with the dialectic of needs and scarce resources; and it always refers to decisions and decision-makers, whether these are individuals, firms, or a community as a whole.

But given the history of economic thought, and given its own present-day consequences, the requirement of a general economic rationality is not self-evident. Apart from the problem of the supposition of limitless needs, the currently dominant thinking appears hard to defend on the question of economic rationality. It accepts, to be sure, that the expansion of needs in an inevitably finite world leads to a general demand for the rationalization of resource allocation. It does not deny that certain allocation decisions inevitably fall outside the market, when the requisites for the market's own smooth functioning are not present. (The problem of the divisibility of exchanged utilities is especially important here, as it is hard to assign a price to the effects of an industrial programme upon the atmospheric pollution of an urban agglomeration, because all its residents are collectively affected.) The dominant way of thinking, then, recognizes that such allocation decisions have to be organized in a different way – through what it rightly calls the political process rather than through market exchange. Yet it still maintains that the only intellectually conceivable type of economic rationalization is the one characteristic of market economy, and even that this market economy is one and the same as the requirement of rationality. It therefore excludes political decisions on resource allocation from the purview of rationalization. In other words, it separates out two areas of decision in the allocation of resources: one that depends upon the market process, whose rules of rationalization are provided by micro-economic theory on the basis of competition and the price system; and one that depends upon the political process, which, though considered perfectly legitimate and even necessary, is presented as incurably arbitrary and 'unrationalizable' because it cannot be based upon an 'independent' system of prices.

Not much more is needed to justify the greatest possible expansion of the sphere of market. After all, 'common sense' tells us that only flesh-and-blood individuals are capable of feeling genuine needs. And even if some needs are called 'collective' for technical reasons of indivisibility, are they not in the end felt and expressed by individuals?

These neoliberal positions, especially characteristic of the American 'public choice' school,[3] ultimately rest upon philosophical options in favour of individualism which go well beyond the field of economic rationalization, and are therefore difficult to discuss in that context. For my part, I would simply like to make the following points.

- The above approach is hard to square with the actual political debate taking place in most countries today, which relates to the qualities of society that people wish to promote in the future. Is it reasonable, for example, to confine the debate on social justice and the associated allocation of scarce resources within a simple perspective of re-electing or not re-electing those who make the decisions – as Joseph Schumpeter, Anthony Downs and Gordon Tullock (one of the founders of the 'public choice' school) have each supposed?[4]
- The global economic, social and ecological constraints of development and modernity impose today, more than ever, a rigorous form of economic rationalization that is not confused with the 'arbitrariness' allegedly inseparable from the sphere of politics.
- Consequently, even if the methodological difficulties are formidable, we must try to find rules for a more general rationalization of resource allocation decisions, including in areas where market mechanisms are not applicable.

SOLVENCY AND PROFITABILITY

The principles of market rationality apply to the behaviour of both buyers and sellers. Since prices are determined anonymously through the overall interaction of supply and demand, the buyer can appear on the market only within the limits of his purchasing power and in

competition with all other buyers. As to the seller, he is in competition
with other sellers and must therefore produce as efficiently as possible
– which means, calculated in terms of the price system, as profitably as
possible. Solvency and profitability are thus two sides of the same
requirement. Both of them appear to be intrinsically linked with competition, but in reality competition is peculiar to the market economy
alone, whereas the twofold requirement applies much more widely to
any economic behaviour, even when competitive conditions are not
present.

Let us take *solvency* first. Theory shows that a solution to the
economic problem implies resource allocation on the basis of priority
objectives, and that a particular choice assumes renunciation of other
conceivable uses of the same resources: this is what economists call the
'opportunity cost'. In any community involved in exchange, economic
choices are possible only if those who make the decisions have the
necessary means to finance them – that is, are 'solvent' – and if they
forgo alternative allocations of the 'scarce' resources (too scarce, that is,
to satisfy all the needs expressed).

Such solvency is considered the basic rule of market economy, whose
twin engines are profit and 'solvent individual demand'. The individual
decision-maker (a physical person or a firm) can engage in market
exchange only if he has sufficient purchasing power (from income or
wealth) to pay the going market price. But the previous line of argument, with its general reference to the tension between needs and
scarcity, allows us to go further. The solvency requirement applies more
generally, in slightly different ways, at the level of the community;
scarcity also compels the community to be 'solvent', so that its economic
choices can be implemented only if it has the means with which to
carry out its objectives. This is why the state, or any other public body
or private association not active on the market, draws up a budget
comparing its revenue and expenditure: its total spending cannot exceed the sums available from all sources (equity capital or reserves,
membership contributions, taxes and loans – although the state's ability
to print money raises special questions that cannot be discussed here).
Solvency of the decision-maker is therefore a general economic rule,
not one bound up only with market assumptions.

The same is true, of course, of the requirement of *efficiency* on the
part of the seller who combines factors of production in order to offer
a product on the market – once it is accepted that there is a problem
of relative scarcity of the factors (labour, raw materials, land, machinery,
production techniques, infrastructural equipment, financial capital,

information, etc.), such that they are not available in sufficient quantity for the needs expressed. Now, as we have seen, this is precisely what defines the most general problem of economics, independent of the assumptions that make the market relation possible. No doubt such scarcity can be deliberately generated – through the artificial creation of needs – but this does not in any way change the requirement of maximum efficiency in the use of the scarce resources.

What is peculiar to the market, however, is that it enables efficiency to be checked in terms of *profitability*. This is possible because a firm can sell its product on a competitive market only if its production costs (and therefore the minimum selling price it can agree without incurring a loss) are equal or inferior to those of its competitors – in which case, profitability is proportional to productive efficiency. A public authority that improves roads or builds schools, however, is not directly exposed to competition; more important, it does not sell its product, so that this cannot be 'profitable' in financial terms. The principle seems simple enough, but its applications are sometimes less so. They are also poorly understood in the debate on privatization and nationalization. For example, a public transport corporation that is required to offer a service accessible to all, or to keep loss-making routes open in sparsely inhabited areas, cannot be 'profitable', and indeed has to be in receipt of subsidies – which does not at all mean that it should be run 'inefficiently'. But this only goes to show the practical advantages of the market!

The answer to the problem of public economic solvency does not involve any special technical difficulty, so long as there is sufficient information about the cost factors. The difficulties are, rather, political in nature, since the resource scarcity entails that choices have to be made between different objectives, and therefore between different interests in the community. This explains, for example, why national development plans (no longer as fashionable as they were) often look more like a 'list of demands' than a medium-term budget.[5] On the other hand, the measuring of efficiency may become technically difficult when it cannot base itself, or cannot base itself exclusively, upon calculations of profitability; for it then requires the elaboration of performance indicators for each specific problem (more jobs, more leisure or more policemen as the most effective solution to the problem of security in the suburbs?), and this may, of course, also become the occasion for indirect political slippage.

CONCLUSION: TOWARDS A MIXED ECONOMY

Doctrinaire proponents of both the market and the state fail to see the complexity of the societies born of modernity. These societies can no longer make do with one-sided criteria: everything we have said so far shows the profound inadequacy of an economic rationality based only upon the market; and evidently a similar argument could be made for a rationality based only upon the state.

The conclusion seems inescapable: our complex societies require a complex system of criteria which combines market mechanisms and collective processes. In what proportions? That remains to be seen, but it, too, depends on political debate rather than on purely technical considerations. Let us end with the provisional principle that *a mixed economy must be mixed both on the demand side and on the supply side*. Demand can no longer be assessed simply from the market expression of solvent individual demand; it is vitally important that other ways of expressing social needs are also recognized. Consequently, supply cannot be limited to the output of profitable production – and if it is not to be so limited, institutional rules have to be set so that collective producers (public or non-public) are able to engage in efficient and socially useful activities without incurring losses, even if those activities are not profitable.

PART TWO

PROBLEMS OF MODERNITY

FROM THE GENERAL LOGIC
TO THE SPECIFIC PROBLEMS

Chapters 2 to 5 started out from a very general survey of the main economic and social changes that took place in the second half of the twentieth century. This revealed both some positive elements and some negative ones, and posed the question of whether the two were inseparable from each other, or whether the latter were inevitable consequences of the former. In order to give an answer, we outlined an analysis of these changes, and tried to link them with the expansion of a system of economic and social organization that claims to be global in reach. This system, which may be termed 'modernity', has its main historical roots in the Enlightenment and the West European Industrial Revolution; but the present changes, taking place within a neoliberal ideological framework, are perhaps deviations from that initial movement.

In order to grasp the nature and evolution of modernity, we first tried to identify its inner logic by analysing its most fundamental characteristics (individualism and the dominance of economics) and by showing how their history is governed by cumulative interaction. Conspicuously placed at the centre of this analysis was the market relation. The study of its mechanisms originally gave rise to the science of economics, but this science, as it has subsequently developed, provides at best only a partial explanation of the events we can observe. Since, however, it claims to be both comprehensive and normative in character, it has eventually given the market relation – and capitalism itself – a decisive importance in the construction of the social system and its prospects for development. While equipping itself with narrow rules of rationality geared solely to a profit criterion that is hardly appropriate for the complex issues at stake in society, modernity has fused with a promise of social progress that is none other than the generalization of market society itself.

Such is the general logic. But the coexistence of positive and negative elements naturally raises some crucial questions about the viability of such a contradictory system, and even more about its prospective generalization. In Part Two we must therefore now turn from theoretical analysis at the level of principles, and explore some of the major challenges thrown up by the future prospects for the system. Of course, we can make no claim to exhaustive treatment of these problems, and will in fact concentrate on five particular areas: growth, inequality, work and employment, international trade, and the role of the public authorities.

CHAPTER 6

THE QUESTION OF GROWTH

Such is the internal contradiction which every oppressive system carries within itself like a seed of death; it is made up of the opposition between the necessarily limited character of the material bases of power and the necessarily unlimited character of the race for power considered as a relationship between men.

Simone Weil, *Oppression and Liberty*, pp. 75–6.

This tendency for the potter to become the slave of his clay…

Arnold Toynbee, *A Study of History*, p. 32.

OVERVIEW: THE GROWTH TRAP, INDISPENSABLE AND IMPOSSIBLE

Because it is based on a belief in never-ending material progress, but above all because it is structured around the indefinite accumulation of profit, the system of capitalist modernity is intrinsically productivist, and insists on a perspective in which human needs are limitless. It maintains this perspective by ceaselessly creating new needs to ensure its own survival. And to this end it uses all the levers that it seems possible to use: from the satisfaction of essential needs and assistance to the poor, through promotion of the quest for comfort, vigour or social prestige, to the organization of 'copycat' consumerism. In any event, considerations of real social utility never have priority in this promiscuous creation of needs. Even the virtuous 'war on poverty', of which so many national and international leaders like to boast, does not always correspond to the motives that one might imagine.

We have already seen how this system resulted in a logic of indefinite growth, and hence in the endless reproduction of scarcity. But we also need to grasp how the growth imperative eventually set up a vicious circle, a real trap inherent in the dynamic thereby unleashed.

The system needs growth to enable the accumulation of profit, but then it uses all the pretexts (starting with employment creation, as we shall see in a later chapter) to justify this need. The fact is that it simply cannot do without growth: its top people keep dreaming of a return of the thirty-year 'golden age',[1] but give way to panic when growth tails off for reasons they cannot control; more seriously (and here I am talking about the industrialized countries), they refuse any real consideration of a voluntary zero-growth strategy.

Let us not oversimplify. These strategic choices are complex, and the difficulties they raise cannot be cleared away in a few moments. Nevertheless, by making the indefinite quantitative growth of market production a key to its own dynamism and survival, the system of capitalist modernity refrains from taking responsibility for the world's long-term development prospects, since resources are limited and various analyses conclude that man's claim on them may already have gone beyond the bounds of what the ecosystem can tolerate – or, to put it another way, 'the earth's carrying capacity'.[2] The long term is perhaps less long, or anyway less remote, than one thinks.

All things considered, we are indeed led to question the old growth imperative that remains at the centre of all current policies. Market economy, even globalized, is condemned to go on growing. But then the real problem is to know whether such growth will remain possible in the future, despite all the economic, social and ecological obstacles discussed above. North American levels of per capita energy consumption or car ownership, for example, obviously cannot be replicated for a population of six, ten or twelve billion without profoundly challenging the planet's ecobalances, or at least those we know today. Imitative consumerism runs up against the same impossibility, because it impels the productive apparatus to keep generating new and artificial needs whose only function is further to isolate people from one another, and to trigger a further imitative reaction. Yet this vicious circle has been made 'official', if we may put it like that, by what the Third World long considered a synonym for development: namely, 'catching up with' the industrial countries in modes and levels of consumption. Of course, this was and still is the only well-grounded objective – *if* the only possible model of development is the one disseminated by the global system.

In this chapter, we shall examine this growth imperative and the reasons behind it, offer some critical reflections on the obstacles in its path, and consider what means there may be, at least in the long term, of escaping from this one-dimensional perspective. But we should be under no illusion. If the need for change is to be taken seriously, it will require a major turnaround not only in the economic policies and development strategies of most governments and international organizations but also in our ways of thinking, our cultures, our reference values.

WHY THE GROWTH IMPERATIVE?

Without repeating the previous argument in detail, we can easily explain the seemingly 'natural' identification of social progress with economic growth by pointing to the Industrial Revolution in Western Europe, and to the global diffusion of modernity that has marked the last two centuries.[3] Although that revolution was preceded and prepared by a long maturing of ideas, industrialization first expressed itself in an increased capacity to produce and circulate commodities. Thanks to advances in hygiene and medicine, there was also a huge rise in the number of people on earth, and hence in the quantity of material needs. In the individualist context of the times, the goods and services (or 'utilities') that corresponded to those needs were mainly ones that could be individually appropriated, and it was mainly towards these that the new productive capacity generated by the Industrial Revolution was steered.

Not by chance did the early foundations of economic theory - which began to appear at the beginning of the same period – formalize just such an individualist market framework for resource allocation in the production of goods and services, and thus for what seemed an evident materialization of social progress. As we have seen, however, capitalism went much further than this simple formalization of market exchange in response to the growth of needs. Capitalism, of course, based itself upon the key idea of market economy: that the best response to people's needs lies not in altruism but in the pursuit of particular interests. But it made the quest for *indefinite accumulation of profit* the central criterion of economic behaviour – a conflation of the economy of needs with the economy of profit which led it to multiply needs as inherently 'limitless', and to fabricate new needs whenever they might serve its interests. This is how the indefinite quantitative growth (and diversification) of commodity output became its main goal of development, for it was precisely such growth that determined the indefinite accumulation of profit.

An additional factor, to which little attention has been paid, reinforces the growth imperative in this system of ours. The system is called 'capitalism' because – in a context of accelerated and increasingly sophisticated technological progress – *finance capital* is the basis of rising productivity and the accumulation of profit (hence the strategic role of capitalist owners and backers in the growth orientation of economic policy). But attempts have recently been made to show that this central role of capital is more complex than it seems at first sight;[4] that capitalism gave a new dimension to the institution of property. In this account, property is no longer just a right of use (a material right) but a *security* enabling its owner either to issue money or a loan himself, or to borrow from other fundholders (non-material right). As the loan is itself conceived as a source of profit, the borrower is required to return the capital with interest; he thus has no choice but to use the borrowed funds to *increase* production, and thereby raise the increment for repayment. This fundamental injunction of a system that uses borrowing for production and lending for profit explains industrialization and its preference for non-renewable natural resources (especially minerals) over renewable resources linked with the flow of solar energy. Such mineral resources are completely used up in production, but this actually permits a higher rate of growth of overall production (for a limited time, of course), because industry can grow much more rapidly than agriculture – and it is rapid growth of this kind which is required to repay the borrowed capital with interest. If this way of looking at things is correct, it helps to explain the exceptional historical period of the last two centuries, which has broken all records for consumption of the stock of natural resources accumulated over millennia.

This reminder of the mechanism of capitalist expansion allows us to see the *cumulative* character of the growth process, which is its apparent justification but also perhaps its condemnation. For although material progress increases the quantity of goods, and therefore the instruments of human survival, this also increases human needs and necessitates further quantitative growth. If we then add the quest for profit spurred on by competition (and perhaps a more general quest for power), if we consider that an increase in the quantity of goods permits an increase in profit and that this in turn leads to further expansion of productive capacity and output, it is by no means clear who might exert pressure for the process to stop.

As we shall see, there are certainly good reasons why we should want it to stop, and why we should master the ways of making that happen. But the reminder given above, especially by distinguishing the situation of 'rich' countries from that of 'poor' countries, should also help us avoid simplistic notions of a halt to the growth process. For in the 'poor' countries, a sudden ending of growth is obviously unacceptable, so long as the population continues its rapid rise and the average satisfaction of basic needs remains at a very low level. There, vigorous growth of production will probably remain necessary for quite a long period to come, and in many cases the first effort to scale down pressures for economic growth should go into a reversal of demographic trends. In the rich countries, on the other hand – let us say, those which belong to the OECD – the necessity of growth may still be unanimously proclaimed by political and economic leaders on the grounds of employment creation, but this necessity is not at all clear in the long run if one takes into account the virtual stagnation of population figures, the already high consumption of material goods and services, and the many possible improvements in the quality of life that do not depend on an increase in the number of commodities. But perhaps it is because of this very lack of factual evidence that ideology takes over and claims that human needs are limitless, thereby justifying endless artificial creation of new needs that make further growth necessary and multiply the opportunities for profit.

In any event, the growth process is by now so well integrated into the overall mechanisms of economic policy that it is hard to imagine its rapid extrication from them; 'liberation' from the growth imperative, if there is such a thing, can only be progressive, and itself organized over the long term. Nevertheless, the conceivable liberation strategies can vary quite widely, according to the initial situation or the rate of demographic growth in relation to the existing level of satisfaction of human needs.

WHY IS THE REQUIREMENT FOR LIMITLESS GROWTH UNACCEPTABLE?

The arguments against the requirement for limitless growth are, on the one hand, economic and ecological, and, on the other, ethical. Here we shall do no more than briefly summarize them.

Let us first emphasize again that, in this system of ours which is claimed to be globalizing, growth is not a temporary policy for escaping a crisis but an objective corresponding to the very nature of modernity. A requirement of indefinite, limitless growth is thus projected within

an ecosystem that has finite, limited resources. This represents a fundamental contradiction between planetary ecosystem and human productive activity (as the latter is conceived in our economic system), but it
is rarely understood as such. We should therefore now briefly but rather
precisely delineate this contradiction.

We shall be using some of the key terms introduced by Nicholas
Georgescu-Roegen, the Romanian-born economist who proposed the
first general theory on this question.[5] This theory is based on the first
two laws of thermodynamics: the first states that 'man can neither create
nor destroy matter or energy'; the second (also called the 'law of
entropy', in reference to the 'bound' energy that cannot be used or
reused by man) states that 'the entropy (that is, the quantity of bound
energy) of a closed system is constantly growing and that the order of
such a system is constantly being transformed into disorder'. Thus, the
human economic activity of production on the planet earth cannot be
imagined as a closed circuit, as so many economics manuals have
suggested. Rather, it should be represented as an open system – open
to an ecosystem that is itself a closed system and therefore subject to
entropy. The economic process is open because it is essentially a 'throughput' of energy-matter. This irreversible one-way flow may be described
in three phases: it uses the low-entropy energy of the natural resources
of the ecosystem (stock of minerals and flow of solar energy); it combines them in the activity of producing goods and services to meet
people's needs; and it discards into the environment high-entropy waste
that can never be used again.

In order to see what this physics-based view of economics implies,
we must first fully grasp that we are dealing with a combination of
energy and material structure, whose accessibility can be understood
only as a whole and in time. It is not enough to object that the
'reserves' of solar energy are virtually limitless in relation to human
needs – both because that energy must become accessible by being
linked to some material support (plants through photosynthesis, for
example), and because terrestrial matter is itself limited. This is why the
exhaustion of resources that should be of concern to us is a question
not only of 'non-renewable' resources (such as minerals), but also of
resources which, though theoretically renewable, are being rapidly de-
pleted (such as biodiversity or fish stocks).

But the really key point here is that scarcity is ultimately 'rooted' in
the irreversible entropic degradation of overall resources. Because this
energy flow becomes forever unusable – or, if you prefer, inaccessible

in view of the combination of material and temporal resources that access would require – it constitutes a limit to man's economic activity. This scarcity is absolute, unlike the relative scarcities that we shall consider in a moment. It does not depend on which technologies are available at a given time, since the very availability of those technologies is bound up with the laws of physics. The obvious conclusion is that in such a system, where resources are finite, it is not possible to conceive of an indefinitely growing human sphere within the planetary eco-system. In the long run, the postulate of indefinite growth is necessarily absurd.

Yet it is this conception of progress which has prevailed for the last two centuries, and which explains the depletion of the earth's resources (especially its store of minerals) at a historically unprecedented tempo, under the impact of industrialization and commodification geared to the indefinite accumulation of profit. 'Development economists' have recommended such industrialization for all the countries on earth, failing to see that it is absolutely essential to maintain a global balance between agriculture and industry. Moreover, this accelerated depletion is compounded today by the anarchic management of renewable re-sources and, perhaps more, by the uncontrolled accumulation of waste. Hence the growing imbalance of the ecosystem as a whole.

These trends are gradually making people aware of the long-term consequences for mankind, of the fact that it is impossible to generalize a system whose main ambition is precisely to generalize itself. This is the first argument for a questioning of the growth imperative. Yet, in the eyes of those who are responsible for the major decisions, this argument is weakened by the inability of the dominant economics to theorize the overall scarcity of resources – or rather, to distinguish be-tween absolute scarcity (as we have just defined it) and the relative scarcities of which the price system takes account.

The traditional way of reasoning in economics does, to be sure, base itself upon the notion of scarcity – but in a purely comparative sense. It takes into account the scarcity of certain resources in relation to other resources, using this to organize an optimal allocation for the ends in view. But curiously it never takes into account the finite character of these resources in relation to human needs, and therefore their absolute scarcity. In other words – and here we follow Lionel Robbins's classical definition – conventional economic reasoning en-ables unevenly scarce resources to be allocated among alternative ends by virtue of the system of relative prices, but it cannot encompass the macro-level of the economy as a whole, the overall dimension of human activity possible with the available resources, and therefore the 'carrying capacity' of the planetary ecosystem in relation to human activity as a whole. As Herman Daly rightly underlines, the price system is only a system of relative indicators; its 'absolutization' would simply make no sense from the point of view of the allocation of resources. This would seem to point to a perspective of anarchic growth, devoid of any economic principle of regulation.

We shall return to these theoretical issues linked with the overall scarcity of resources. But we should note that the discussion is not purely ecological or theoretical: it also has an ethical dimension; it calls into question a certain conception of man (traditional in economics) as a being whose ambitions are limited to the heedless and ever-increasing consumption of material resources and products, and a conception of social progress as the result of an ever-increasing production of commodities.

In this light, we may now look again at the growth imperative as a particularly good example of the confusion of ends and means. Although it is supposed to furnish the means of social progress, growth becomes in effect an end in itself, an inescapable requirement which ultimately prevails over all other requirements. Herman Daly says in this connection that economists never discuss final goals, or indeed anything absolute, but focus all their attention on the intermediate elements of the 'ends–means continuum' – only some elements, moreover, which can be privately acquired, and therefore made the object of market relations. More specifically, we might say that the reasoning and conceptual tools of the 'traditional' economist project an extraordinarily reductionist image of man as a subject of purely individual needs, to be satisfied through the private acquisition of an ever-growing number of material goods.

The general features of modernity that we began by identifying – individualism and the dominance of market economics – are clearly at the origin of growth-oriented behaviour. But we can now see more clearly than before the fundamentally amoral character of the growth imperative that dominates modernity (that is, its lack of any moral concern for the diversity and legitimacy of needs, their social dimension, their degree of relative urgency). The idea of changing this imperative is therefore not based exclusively on the limited availability of resources; it also involves a profound ethical dissatisfaction with the image of man that it reflects.

HOW CAN WE CHANGE THE GROWTH IMPERATIVE, AND IN THE NAME OF WHICH RATIONALITY?

Let us return to the dimension of human economic activity as a whole in relation to the available resources and the earth's 'carrying capacity', for it is this which is called into question by the indefinite growth imperative. On what do the global dimension and its evolution over a certain period depend? They depend first of all on the size of the population and the quantity of material production that the energy-matter flowing from the store of natural resources places at its disposal; they also depend, of course, on the culture and value systems of the various population groups present in the area, on the level of scientific knowledge and available technology, and on the various institutional and material factors determining how the access to resources is distributed among these groups in society.

In this perspective, those who advocate a gradual orientation of human activity towards 'steady-state economics' believe that it is necessary to stabilize, at least in the long term, the number of people on earth and the volume of their material production, by relying on changes in cultures, values, technologies and modes of distribution. Their reasoning, then, does not abandon the concerns of economic rationality – on the contrary. But it does seek to formulate them in a different, more general way, since the traditional mode of calculation based on the price system is not applicable. In Daly's pioneering work, this new economic rationality is seen as imposing a threefold requirement in relation to the 'throughput' schema mentioned earlier: (a) to maintain as far as possible the previous level of resources; (b) to limit as much as possible the removal of energy from the existing stock; and (c) to improve as much as possible the efficiency of the services performed through withdrawal of energy from this stock.

Georgescu-Roegen went further than this when he explicitly criticized the idea of a steady-state economics that could go on *ad infinitum*. In the long run, he thought, it was indispensable 'to replace the steady state with a decreasing state'.[6] But the implications of this dramatic statement, both for population levels and for living standards, do not seem to have been spelt out. Here we shall not examine the principles involved or the form in which they are presented in detail, but simply consider what they mean for a general policy concerning the growth imperatives of the system of capitalist modernity. Three consequences immediately come to mind:

- The resources of the earth's ecosystem are recognized as absolutely scarce in relation to the uses that human beings can make of them; or, as Georgescu-Roegen puts it, 'The law of entropy is the root of economic scarcity.'[7] Inescapably, therefore, human activity cannot set itself a long-term perspective of limitless growth. Humanity as a whole is subject to certain limits; it cannot continue indefinitely drawing on the resources of the earth's ecosystem to increase the total sum of material production.

- To give up a long-term prospect of limitless overall growth does not mean that all growth has to be proscribed. Some kinds of growth are obviously indispensable – for example, to feed a still growing population whose basic needs have not been met. This means returning to an evident truth of which the system of modernity has lost sight in its confusion of needs-based and profit-based economics: the truth that not all human needs are equally important. In man's quest for material progress and broader 'development', the priority should not – as the present system claims – be aggregate growth. But *selective* growth of areas of production corresponding to what are considered essential needs remains a necessary and perfectly legitimate goal of human activity. And as part of the concern to limit overall depletion, the greater subtraction of global resources required by selective growth should be able to rest upon a reduced subtraction of resources for areas of production considered less of a priority.

- Lastly, of course, there is no getting round the requirement of *efficiency* in the allocation of resources. As this remains true even when the price system is operating badly, or not at all, rules of economic rationality must be found which apply beyond the limits of market situations.

If a policy of undifferentiated growth (pursued for its own sake as an imperative goal) must be replaced by a policy of selective and limited growth (pursued as an important but not exclusive means of social progress), then it is essential that we think of this as a process involving choices – a perspective that political economy should never have abandoned in the first place. Moreover, such a process of choices must be able to draw upon new systems of values, a political rather than purely market-driven expression of needs, and an economic theory broader than just market economics.

We shall return at greater length in the last part of this book to the necessity of a change in values and a different approach to economic theory, because these run right through what is being proposed here.

But we can already say a word or two about the different approach required to the expression of needs.

THE MODE OF EXPRESSION OF NEEDS

It is the social demand rather than the political supply that has to be strengthened.

Alain Touraine, *L'Après-socialisme*, p. 13.

[T]he major choices in society are not made by anyone.

Pierre Bourdieu, *Sur la télévision*, p. 60.

This question deserves a central place in our considerations because, despite the complexity of the many associated issues, it leads on to one of the changes most urgently needed in the system of modernity. Again, the reason for this is evident enough, since the expression of needs shapes the very purpose of economics. The fact that today this seems to be totally forgotten is another sign of the confusion between ends and means that we have already attacked a number of times.

The ethical dimensions of this problem are manifest, and I would like to begin with a profession of faith which will hardly strike anyone as original, but which does not seem to me superfluous in light of the foregoing analysis.

It is my belief that the first aim of all economic and social organization is, or rather should be, to satisfy the priority needs of all men and women, not to permit the accumulation of profit or the maximization of power in the hands of a few. The requirements are, first and foremost, that these needs are given *general* expression; next, that the necessary mediations and priorities are organized in accordance with certain value judgements and overall resource availability; and only lastly that the means to implement these social priorities are worked out in detail through a system of incentives for those with the responsibility for decisions – a system in which individual profit naturally plays a legitimate and important role.

Now, as we know, the mode of economic organization that is spreading in the wake of the neoliberal globalization of modernity confers pride of place on market mechanisms. The only needs whose expression can reach the productive system are, in principle, those of the solvent individual consumer. Through the play of prices and quantities, this mechanism is supposed to lead to general market equilibrium: not only for the consumption goods directly concerned but also, indirectly, for the total of goods, services and factors of production (including labour, capital, technology and entrepreneurship) which come together in the expanding output of society. This system, then, is supposed to reflect the sovereignty of solvent consumers over the totality of resource allocation decisions.

Such is the theoretical schema. As we have seen, it achieves a social 'optimum' only when the conditions of what economists call pure and perfect competition are met – and even this 'optimum' satisfaction of expressed needs remains closely dependent upon the initial distribution of wealth and income, as it is only solvent consumers who have the right to express themselves. There is consumer satisfaction only if there is a profit in it for the supplier. And most often, of course, the supplier has considerable power to manipulate the expression of needs.

In the actual reality of all market economies, things are considerably more complicated. First, certain basic needs cannot easily be ignored, even though the people who feel them cannot express them on the market because they are not solvent. For example, no one dares any longer to argue openly, in the name of some theoretical principle, that the right thing to do is to allow the destitute or the handicapped to starve to death. Second, a number of collective needs (the need for public order, or an officially recognized currency, or a transport infrastructure, for example) affect the functioning of markets, but they seem technically difficult to satisfy through the market path of private appropriation and profit.

No modern organization of the economy is based purely on the market. Always the market is combined with various types of collective intervention – by public bodies, associations, and so on. And the social needs to which these interventions correspond have to make themselves known in one way or another. Such expressions of need therefore exist alongside others asserted by market mechanisms, and it would be wrong to claim that modern societies know nothing except 'market demand'.

All the same, if the interpretation offered here is correct, and the globalization of modernity corresponds to market economic pressure to extend deeper and deeper into the relations of society, then the inevitable coexistence of different modes of the expression of needs does not do away with competition among them. Moreover, such competition constantly works to the advantage of market needs, helping the market and the commodity to extend their supremacy ever further. As we shall see, it is because of this cumulative process of marketization or commodification that we can speak of modernity as 'alienating'.

The process may be observed in specific details. In the mode of social and economic organization that is tending to become general, the dominance of market needs (and hence of the corresponding form of their expression) is becoming more and more pronounced, whereas collective needs are reduced to the status of mere means serving market ends. Everyone's right to freedom and dignity, for example, or the role of health, education, democracy and public cleanliness, is not totally disregarded, because the population will exert as much pressure as it can on its representatives to assume responsibility for these needs. To judge by the decisions of the dominant economic players or international funders, however, the chance that such popular needs will be effectively integrated into a development strategy (that is, an overall schema for the allocation of resources) depends on the extent to which the functioning of the market is thereby made smoother or better. Yes to democracy – so long as it helps to maintain the social equilibrium that the market cannot do without. Yes to better health and education – so long as they help to raise labour productivity. Yes to new means of environmental protection – so long as they help companies survive, and can be made the object of profitable productive activity. But if any collective services fail to have this instrumental character in relation to market activity, if collective demands and market demands compete rather than complement each other, then the brute facts reassert themselves and the market has all the chances of victory on its side.

Furthermore, numerous collective goods or services do not have the privilege of being potentially compatible with the market; the creation of green spaces and long-term reforestation, for example, or making great works of culture accessible to the public, attract scarcely any interest from investors. As to income inequality, it may appear morally regrettable to most people – but after all, let's be realistic, it usually boosts the level of aggregate savings and the production of certain luxury or semi-luxury goods, and for companies it is doubtless more profitable to produce private cars by the thousand than buses by the hundred. Many more examples could be given, but the conclusion already seems clear: the market (with its criteria of solvency, profitability and competitiveness) is the final arbiter of needs to which all other expressions are subordinate.

It is this subordinate position that must be changed. This is not to say that needs expressed on the market should become suspect or illegitimate – only that their claim to absolute supremacy should be denied, so that a different, complementary balance is struck between market and non-market modes of the expression of needs, in accordance with a different hierarchy of social needs that has still to be defined.

A number of practical consequences follow from this. The first is that responsibility for meeting the needs of society should be institutionally shared between market players and non-market players. The proportions obviously cannot be decided *a priori*, and will vary according to context; what is important is that this division of responsibility should be on a basis of systematic complementarity – not, as it is today, on a basis of subordination. The criterion for this sharing is a matter for choice in the general interest; it cannot be left up to the arbitrary decision of private interests. Such complementarity should thus be a task for the various institutions of society to achieve, and should not be left to the relationship of forces between the various interests present in the arena, as neoliberal doctrine maintains.

The second consequence is that modes of expression other than solvent demand must be given back all their practical importance – through encouraging the utmost individual initiative outside the circuits of money (for example, the neighbourly 'exchange of services' that it would certainly not be desirable to 'commodify' to the maximum[8]), but above all through encouraging the initiative of 'non-profit organizations'. More generally, all the parties concerned – individuals, associations and social movements, as well as public authorities at various levels – should be urged to change their approach radically, and to treat modes of expressing needs sidelined by market demand as equally genuine (that is, as equally authoritative expressions of social needs).

It is crucially important that public authorities should expand and strengthen their means of observing social reality within a perspective defined by the public interest, even if this reality is not expressed in orthodox macroeconomic and macrofinancial indicators. This should involve new types of analysis and new indicators, based especially on opinion surveys and on systematic study of the most significant social facts (modes of consumption, prestige goods, crazes for a particular public figure, religious movements, migrations). But it should also involve analysis of social dysfunctionalities and resulting forms of violence, as well as the testimony of artists, intellectuals and all other kinds of 'disinterested' observers (disinterested in the sense that their aim in expressing the state of society is not that of seeking new market openings). Such a deepening and widening of the study of the future of society should be backed up with expert reports on the most difficult areas that it brings to light. Here is fertile ground indeed for the activity of economists and sociologists.

In short, in the face of the socially suicidal reductionism of the market approach, there is a burning need for fresh and imaginative thinking to identify the needs of society. We should also note, however – as France's former environment minister Corinne Lepage did in relation to the media silence following the Kyoto conference[9] – that the pressure of scientists, and more generally of citizens and public opinion, can play a considerable role in expanding the ways in which social needs are recognized.

One last but not unimportant point. We should not forget that the 'economic imperative' remains in force because of the scarcity of means in relation to most needs expressed, although this should not be confused with the 'profitability imperative'. For collective needs, the solvency rule no longer applies to individuals taken separately, but it does still hold for the community as such. Beyond the recognized modes of expressing social needs, some judgement has to be made between them in accordance with the resources that the community is actually prepared to devote to their satisfaction (the principle of 'revealed preferences', to use economists' jargon). It is necessary to 'listen' to society, but this is not enough – for society or its representatives must eventually settle the matter. While politics should not be enslaved to economics, nor can it simply ignore it. This is another of those evident truths which are masked by the character of the debate in society.

Let us now sum up the first consequence that the questioning of growth implies for the expression of needs. If the economy is to serve the needs that society makes its priority, society must be better aware of the imbalance in the present situation; it must regain control of the expression and arbitration of those needs, and no longer allow market mechanisms and the particular interests that profit from them to exercise a monopoly in this regard.

Such an emancipation requires a radical change in the very logic of modernity, and of its neoliberal globalization. And because of this, it conflicts not only with the prevailing alienation but also with the interests that dominate this society and the concepts they employ.

CONCLUSION

We have seen that some forms of growth remain indispensable to humanity, but that any conflation of development or social progress with limitless aggregate growth should be roundly rejected. The constant recommendations of short-term growth must be left behind, because they lead to a long-term impossibility. The long term, in fact, begins today. Moreover, if we look beyond the most powerful interests that make up the present constellation, it is the very logic of the system of modernity that is in question. Unless this is gradually but profoundly transformed, the marginal corrections designed to mitigate the harmful effects of growth will not be sufficient to solve the problem.

CHAPTER 7

EQUITY AND INEQUALITIES

Social distribution and not growth would dominate the politics of the new millennium.

Eric Hobsbawm, *The Age of Extremes*, p. 577.

INTRODUCTION: ECONOMIC DEVELOPMENT AND SOCIAL DEVELOPMENT

Our analysis of the limitless growth imperative, which seems inseparable from the dominant model of development, has just enabled us to identify a first major impasse in this model: the impossibility of generalizing it to the whole of the planet, for reasons connected with natural resources and the equilibrium of ecosystems. But a study of its recent history throws up a second set of objections that result in a second impasse. These concern the social equilibrium and, more broadly, the 'social development' – a term that has become popular since the 1995 UN Summit on the question in Copenhagen – of societies which organize themselves, or think they can organize themselves in the future, according to the rules of the dominant model.

However, the link between this second set of objections and the dominant model of development is not obvious at first sight, and their integration into the analysis poses a basic problem that requires some brief explanation.

The difficulty stems, first of all, from the impreciseness of the definitions, and above all from the multiplicity of components, in what are known as 'social equilibrium' and 'social development'. What exactly is involved? Distribution of the costs and benefits of the growth and development process, and especially of the resulting income? Conformity to a more or less precise norm of social justice in such distribution, and

73

if so which norm? Reference to various 'social indicators' such as those developed over the last decade by the UNDP to measure the level and the quality of life? Social mobility, and opportunities for social advancement? Greater appreciation of the harmony observable in relations among social groups, and maintenance or improvement of all the mechanisms on which this harmony depends? An overall assessment of the degree of integration and cohesion within a particular society?

Answers to these questions call for both a definition of terms and a political debate. Obviously, a number of different ways of looking at things are both possible and defensible, but the development of real dialogue and real policies requires that the relevant community should agree on one or several approaches. Thus, the organizers preparing for the Copenhagen Summit made the far from arbitrary proposal (in fact, it involved a serious judgement about the priorities of the day) that the consideration of 'social development' should concentrate on three areas or problems: poverty, unemployment, and the more general issue of social integration.

But the main obstacle to a conceptually and politically satisfactory approach to social development is not terminological; it is located much more deeply within the economic logic of the dominant model itself, and is therefore closely bound up with the critique offered in this work. Let us briefly try to demonstrate this.

The model of neoliberal modernity is dominated by individualism and economism. Its basic drive to expand is organized around market exchange (solvent demand and profit maximization), the indefinitely rising production of commodities, and the accumulation of profit through the production and ever-increasing circulation of commodities and capital. It is in this sense that the model is essentially economic in nature − although it governs the evolutionary logic of the whole of society. What place, then, should be given to the issues of *social* equilibrium and *social* development? At first sight the answer would appear to be 'none', since these concerns are not necessary. The doctrine underlying the dominant model maintains that the economic mechanisms of the market and accumulation ensure 'optimal' convergence between the pursuit of profit and the satisfaction of the needs of society as a whole. It soon becomes clear, however, that even if the highly restrictive conditions for such convergence are met, the optimum can never be any more than relative; for the 'ideal' solution is the best only in relation to the initial distribution of purchasing power − that is, of wealth and income. This is why a social dimension has to be introduced into the overall evaluation. But as one might expect in a mode of functioning dominated by market mechanisms, this social dimension mainly concerns matters linked with the distribution of income. By taking it into account, one is able to make a number of corrections deemed desirable to the market outcome (through redistributive measures involving tax-and-transfer, as well as the provision of public goods and services in place of marketized production), when the market fails to satisfy certain needs recognized as socially important. But such action is always essentially corrective. In the liberal (and especially the neoliberal) philosophical underpinnings of modernity, the market nevertheless retains its central place as the mechanism allocating resources and regulating the whole of society. The role of the public authorities and (at least until recently) the so-called 'informal' sector in less modernized countries is not denied, but it is certainly considered subordinate to that of the market. And, more generally, this subordination affects all the mechanisms of social regulation that are not directly tied to the market. Their role may be tolerated, sometimes even welcomed as a complement averting imbalances that might disturb the smooth operation of the market. But no challenge is tolerated to the dominance of the market as the organizational principle in society.

This is the context in which we must understand the ambivalent relationship between the 'economic' and the 'social' dimensions of capitalist modernity. As we know, the essence of this modernity is economic: the market mechanism is supposed to solve, in the best way possible, all the problems of society deriving from the scarcity of resources. Non-market interventions are accepted only as a back-up, or sometimes as a corrective, and then within narrow limits. This is not only for liberal philosophical reasons, but also because the very logic of the market is totalitarian, and its cohesion would be threatened by the large number of 'distortions' inevitably accompanying any other mode of resource allocation. Economic theory (or, at least, the theory underlying the model) states that the market permits the most efficient allocation of resources, and hence the fastest growth of the total product; problems of distributive justice, if they are posed at all, should be resolved only as matters of secondary importance, and should not be allowed to interfere with the market mechanism. At the end of the day, it is easier to tackle problems of distribution after the 'cake' has been made as large as possible.

Once it has put the choice between efficiency and equity into this kind of perspective, the dominant ideology can emphasize the dichotomy, and especially the hierarchy, between 'the economic' and 'the social'. After all, the real problems of development and progress are economic in nature, and so the main concerns should be the conditions of production, the division of labour, trade, efficiency (equated with profitability), and the accumulation of capital and profit; all the rest are extras. To be sure, progress has its costs. In the market form of organization – which history is supposed to have shown to be more efficient than collective organization – it even entails nothing short of warfare, as a result of the inevitable rivalry and competition among individual players. Of course, this means there are winners and losers: how could it be otherwise? There can be no question of giving up the principle of economic warfare, because this is simply the implementation of the principle of competition. The battlefields may be strewn with dead and wounded, but the generals will send an ambulance to give first aid to those who have some chance of pulling through.[1] Thus, if this really is the general framework, the sharpness of the paradox can hardly be disguised: today's 'social development' is this ambulance sent to the battlefield of an economic war that no one is either able or willing to abandon.

Let us simply add that this paradox can be denied only by those who refuse to seek the causes of this need for 'social development' – not so much the immediate causes of particular inadequacies as the structural, systemic causes of the split between the economic and the social. We shall later find the same paradox in the 'war on poverty' – an unconvincing slogan, much bandied about by international organizations and aid agencies, which stems from the same refusal to go beyond symptoms and to identify the systemic causes of the phenomena that one claims to be combating.

In economic policy and development strategy, this kind of dissociation of the economic and the social is clearly the source of numerous confusions on the level of both vocabulary and content. What justification is there for saying that commodity-producing activities such as industry or agriculture are 'economic', whereas the health and education sectors are held to be 'social'? Why does the question of wages and salaries belong to the realm of the 'social', whereas the question of dividends remains bound up with an 'economic' approach? Why have restructuring programmes systematically made a priority of macroeconomic and macrofinancial equilibria, and concerned themselves with social equilibria only when rioting or the threat of civil disorder has forced the Bretton Woods institutions to introduce a 'social adjustment' dimension?

One could go on endlessly with such questions, and no doubt elements of a 'common-sense' answer could be found to some of them. It might be argued, for instance, that 'people' are more directly involved in wages or education, in comparison with the administration of 'things' such as industrial dividends or the affairs of a bank. But that kind of argument will convince only those who deny that economics is, in the end, a matter of individuals, social groups and human communities. Nor is this simply a semantic dispute, for a more integrated approach is indispensable if the wide range of questions are to be answered. The demand for such an approach does not stem principally from an academic concern for intellectual consistency; it derives from the fact that the split between the economic and the social necessarily entails a difference in the way problems are handled, and this necessary difference serves to justify political leaders when they systematically sacrifice social criteria to economic criteria on the grounds that the latter dictate an 'optimal' allocation of development resources.

This demand for an approach that coherently integrates the economic and social dimensions of development is the central challenge facing 'social development' today. It has already given rise to a considerable number of works, especially in the last few years, but the solution still seems a long way off.

I do not claim to offer a solution here, but I shall try to start the process of reflection by exploring two 'social' components of the present state of the world economy. These two themes − which are chosen for their intrinsic importance, of course, but also because they seem directly bound up with the logic of neoliberal modernity − are *the growth of inequalities* and (in Chapter 8) *the future of work*.

THE SHARPENING OF INEQUALITIES

Again, taking the global perspective which is implicit in the model of economic liberalism, inequalities of development are irrelevant unless it can be shown that they produce globally more negative than positive results.
Eric Hobsbawm, *The Age of Extremes*, p. 573.

Inequality, or why are there rich and poor? This is truly the key question of economics.
Pierre-Noël Giraud, *L'Inégalité du monde*, p. 9.

No one today denies that the sharpening of inequalities is one of the most spectacular recent trends in modernity.[2] But it is not one that is easy to interpret. The first difficulty (even if we restrict ourselves to income inequality) is the very complexity of the phenomenon: complexity of the measurement of inequality (which income groups should we compare without falsifying the overall picture?); complexity of the forms of inequality (between capital and labour, or between different skill groups of workers); complexity of the constants and variables of inequality throughout history; complexity of the possible mechanisms of fighting against inequalities, and of the different theoretical analyses on which they rest.

We shall return to some of these problems, but the general interpretation also presents some difficulty. Following on from some of our previous observations, we can immediately note the major (and rather surprising) contrast between these inequalities and the productiveness of capitalist modernity. Never before in history has an economic system produced such wealth, accumulated and invested so much, been capable of sustaining such strong growth over such a long time. In any historical comparison, the performance of the capitalist system is truly exceptional, even if growth in the industrialized countries is no longer what it was during the three decades following the Second World War.

In the face of such evidence, it might be tempting to argue that quantitative advances of such magnitude cannot take place everywhere at once, and that temporary inequalities among people are a kind of inevitable ransom that has to be paid for them. Certainly most of the leading economic figures, both nationally and internationally, still proclaim – at least in public – a philosophy of equal opportunity according to which the weakest will eventually 'catch up' with the strongest. Indefinitely rising incomes and living standards do still seem to be the main objective in relation to all strata of world society.

Yet the world has never before known such profound inequalities. Many countries in the South have, it is true, seen their income progress much faster than that of the industrial heartlands, and the gap as measured by the main social indicators (life expectancy at birth, for example) has been narrowing considerably. The fact remains, however, that differences between countries are still very great, and that the gaps between social groups within countries (especially the richer countries) have grown sharply in recent decades, and worsened the plight of the least privileged strata. According to official calculations made by international organizations, the world has never had so many human beings living below the recognized 'poverty threshold'; forms of extreme poverty (starvation and disease, as well as the sequels of war and population displacement) have never been spread among so many people; and the richest countries are themselves witnessing a spectacular return of poverty, exclusion and marginalization, with huge income disparities between the very rich and the very poor.

So what has happened? And what is likely to happen? Let us first briefly make a few things clear.

In the eighteenth century, before the Industrial Revolution, 'the world was still a world of equal entities, in the sense that the average standard of living was roughly the same in Europe, India and China, the three most populous areas of the planet', even though 'the gap between rich and poor was considerable inside them'.[3] From the eighteenth century until approximately 1970, there was a dual tendency for inequalities to spread between countries, and – at least towards the end – to diminish within countries. Over the long term, as American economist Simon Kuznets has shown (with his famous inverted 'U curve' representing the evolution of inequalities), economic growth seems to go together with an increase and then a reduction of inequality within the growth economies.

In the last thirty years or so, however, this dual internal and international tendency has been *reversed*. Part of the Third World has started a process of catching up with the income levels of the richest countries – first in the 'newly industrializing countries' of East Asia, then (at least until the last few years) in much more populous countries such as China, India, the former USSR, Eastern Europe and even parts of Latin America – whereas other countries (especially in Africa) have been sinking into stagnation and dire poverty. But at the same time, social inequalities have increased considerably within most countries (especially the richer ones), taking the form of unemployment in Europe and pay inequality in the United States. Thus, in its 1997 *World Development Report*, the UNDP showed that if the per capita income of the richest 20 per cent are compared with that of the poorest 20 per cent, the ratio today is an average of 8 to 1 in the developing countries (19 to 1 in Latin America), but also 7 to 1 in the richest countries. Thomas Piketty, drawing on the work of Drèze and Sen, has shown – with a slightly different method of calculation – that the gap of 1 to 10 between the Westerner of 1870 and the Westerner of 1990 is 'roughly the same, or even slightly smaller, than the gap between the average income of a Chinese or Indian in 1990 and the average income of a Westerner in 1990, according to the best available estimates for purchasing power parity'.[4]

Economists have given various explanations for these tendencies (technological progress, migration and competition linked with globalization, inevitable transitional effects of trade liberalization), but Pierre-Noël Giraud considers them to be 'unconvincing', and insists that this is a critical problem for economics. The general proposals for action to remedy the inequalities are even less convincing, for – as we have already noted – the 'war on poverty' slogan that always crops up in aid strategies never goes beyond the symptoms to tackle the root causes.[5] Without going into the details of a particularly complex debate, let us at least draw out some elements that are crucial for an overall interpretation.

The core of this interpretation must be sought at the level of the system. In the short term, of course, we can (and should) tend, in a thousand ways, the wounds of poverty and inequality. But no action of that kind makes sense in the long run unless we grasp that the operation of the market – for all its qualities and the dynamic growth it permits – is intrinsically a mechanism for the cumulative strengthening of inequalities, especially once it becomes the dominant mechanism of social regulation. This is so because the operation of the market is based upon solvent demand, whose structure is in the end determined by the initial distribution of wealth and income. Unequal distribution at the start is the source of power disparities in the operation of the market itself, and hence of a cumulative intensification of inequalities. When the dominant economic theory speaks the language of 'optimum' and 'optimization' – and especially when it studies the functioning of the market in the highly restrictive conditions of 'pure and perfect competition' – its reasoning is based upon a 'given' initial distribution. The optimum it identifies is therefore relative (its more serious theorists have never pretended otherwise). But what is worse is that the very achievement of this optimum cumulatively strengthens the causes that make it relative.

CORRECTIVE ACTION?

Is it possible to counteract this cumulative increase of inequalities? Various kinds of public redistribution in the general interest may be identified; 'pure redistribution', for example, has been distinguished from 'efficient redistribution'. Pure redistribution concerns situations in which the market is functioning at its best, and yielding what economists call a 'Pareto optimum': that is, an outcome which can be improved for some only if the satisfaction for others is reduced. It is therefore possible to change this outcome for reasons of social justice, either through direct action on the price system (for example, by ordering an increase in certain categories of workers' wages) or through tax-and-transfer policy (for example, by taxing large salaries and capital gains at a higher rate). Effective redistribution, by contrast, operates in situations where the market cannot yield a Pareto optimum because the mechanisms of competition are distorted (for example, if elements of monopoly or oligopoly are present); intervention then more directly targets the conditions of the production process (especially, as we shall see, the institutions that set the rules for the production process). The differences between these two forms of redistribution are considerable, but they stem from differences in the situations to which they apply, rather than from the scale of the intended redistributive effects.

Similarly, it is important to distinguish the forms of redistribution applicable between the rewards of capital and labour from the forms applicable between the pay of workers with different skill levels. In both cases, the operation of the market can be understood only if we consider the margins of choice that are technologically open. Can quantities of equipment and quantities of labour, or quantities of labour at different skill levels, be combined in variable proportions? Or are these quantities linked to each other, at least in the short term, by fixed coefficients?

Thomas Piketty shows that, over the short term, the diversity of these starting conditions leads to profoundly different possibilities, demands and strategies of redistribution, and to sharply contrasting results. (The position of unskilled labour, for example, has been much more important in the United States than in Europe, with lower pay but higher levels of employment.) But he also argues that over the long term (1920–95 for the USA, France and Britain) the distribution of corporate added value shows a surprisingly regular proportion of a third for capital and two-thirds for labour – a finding, moreover, which raises the thorny problem of interpreting the significance of 'social struggles' in the long run if they remain limited to this issue of distribution.

I shall not enter further into these complexities of the analysis of inequality. My aim here is simply to recall that they exist, both in theory and in practice, and that we cannot therefore treat the analysis as perfectly simple and straightforward. But let us return to the main argument. What makes it difficult to understand such situations, and to devise ways of acting in relation to them, is of course the large number of variables that have to be taken into account. It is precisely this complexity which encourages recourse to the relatively 'spontaneous' mechanism of the market. Yet the market does no more than register and develop the initial inequalities of power, and the operation of the market mechanism can, in the best of cases, lead to an 'effective', but not necessarily a 'just', result.

The problem, then, is to know how to act in terms of justice, without diminishing the result in terms of effectiveness. This is the main difficulty used to justify the dominant approach, which defines efficiency as 'economic' and distribution as 'social', and keeps the two quite separate from each other, with the result that the rules of economic development can never be changed, however damaging they may be, because the market is a 'natural' institution, and the aim of 'social development' is precisely to repair the damage without attacking its causes. This almost schizophrenic dissociation, presented as a split between two contradictory logics, is enough to explain the impotence of the Copenhagen Summit.

The conclusion must be that the market mechanism, though indispensable, is not always effective, and – from the point of view of justice – does not by itself ensure a satisfactory outcome. If it is accepted that social justice is an objective no less important than growth, then the market cannot be the only mechanism; it must be combined with other ways of influencing the economy and the distribution of its product. The difficulty is to imagine an 'integrated' mode of functioning – not economic warfare followed by social distribution, but *a mixed economy combining efficiency and equity*, through a mix of market regulation and collective regulation. But although the idea of such a mixed economy is clear enough, we have to admit that its actual forms in each situation have still largely to be invented.

It should be added that globalization – a tendency that began with capitalism itself, but has accelerated over the last two decades – is strengthening the effects of the market mechanism. By making the various elements of the world economy more interdependent, it throws the mechanisms of inequality into sharper relief. But here again, we must not content ourselves with simplistic explanations. In the industrialized countries, for example, imports from low-wage areas do not, today, make up a sufficiently large part of total consumption to explain a general tendency for wages to decline. Indeed, low wages in many so-called developing countries may themselves be the source of a general development standstill in those same countries, as they endeavour to find in exports a solvent demand for products which they cannot sell on an impoverished internal market. Thus, in order to increase their competitiveness on external markets, they try to bring about the decline (or prevent the rise) of their national production costs, especially wage costs, and this reduces still further the scope for sales inside the country. Clearly, as this kind of mechanism becomes more widespread, it reduces total world demand, at least in some sectors, giving rise to the various cases of overproduction that are a feature of today's world economy.

Unless global pressures for profit maximization and more intense competition are corrected by some worldwide public intervention, they have the effect of making some poorer and others richer. Opponents of globalization, in making their case, may thus counter its ostensible advantages by referring to the new poverty it brings about (especially through the destruction of local economies and the refusal to prioritize the essential needs of the population). The more radical among them even go so far as to argue that 'we would perhaps be better off if the whole of the world trade system collapsed'.[6]

As the logic of an overall system, then (rather than because of any particular components), neoliberal globalization is a major source of the sharpening of inequalities. It is not adequate to explain these inequalities by reference to each local situation; structural determinants must also be taken into account in what is, after all, a worldwide tendency.

Naturally, this analysis is contested by the leading globalizers – particularly by the international finance organizations and, in their wake, most of the other international organizations – even if this involves them in some striking contradictions. In its 1997 report (which was nevertheless a critical document), the UNDP could admit that 'globalization has its winners and its losers', and then, a few lines later, claim that 'inequality is not inherent in globalization'.[7]

Finally, let us note another complexity in the impact of our economic and social system on inequalities: namely, the ambivalent positions that are taken on the subject. This affects what might be called the evolution of the 'inequality toleration threshold', both in the general public and among political leaders. For as we have seen, although official development strategies continue to speak of equality, in the early 1990s Galbraith was already analysing a 'culture of contentment' among the middle-class majority in the United States which was able to shift and modify government policies.[8] Some have seen in this not only a deformation bound up with capitalist modernity, but an *anti-egalitarian consensus* that is the other side of the coin of a mass adherence to the principles (or myths) of free enterprise, liberalization and globalization, as well as a fatalistic resignation to their social costs.[9]

No doubt this consensus still prevails in the United States. It may be in the process of weakening in Western Europe, although the recent political changes are still too new and too uncertain to confirm or invalidate this judgement. Some recent tendencies in Asia – and also in

Latin America, where the tradition of inequality is much stronger – should be examined within the same perspective, as should the at least formal persistence of democratic demands more or less everywhere in the world. In any event, it is no longer possible to ignore the problem of the relationship between the spread of capitalist modernity and the sharpening of inequalities.

CHAPTER 8

WORK AND EMPLOYMENT

Here, then, are the heart of the problem and the heart of the conflict. The point is to disconnect from 'work' the right to have rights – especially the right to what is and can be produced without work, or with less and less work. The task before us is to realize that neither the right to an income, nor full citizenship, nor the blossoming and identity of each individual, can any longer revolve around whether he or she has a job – and to change society in accordance with that realization.

André Gorz, *Misères du présent, richesse du possible*, pp. 90–91.

A NEW AND CONTRADICTORY SITUATION

Should any of our descendants, a few decades or a few centuries from now, feel curious enough to read what our present government advisers are saying about macroeconomic policy, they may be fascinated by their virtuosity in manipulating highly abstract statistical aggregates. But they will surely not fail to ask a seemingly naive question: where are men and women in all of this?

Even if employment still serves as a pretext for growth in the discourse of most political leaders, even if the solvency of individual consumers is still the basis of market expansion, there have been a number of signs in recent years that a fundamental change is taking place in the functioning and perspectives of the economic organization of modernity. This change affects the place that is ultimately reserved for the main interested parties: that is, for living people, or, to be more precise, for their work.

Why are the radical 'metamorphoses of the wage-earning society'[1] occurring at the very moment when it seemed finally to have triumphed after a long and arduous ascent? Why are these transformations such a serious threat to the future of our societies?

Why does the 'end of work' – perhaps overdramatized in some projections,[2] much more convincing in others[3] – seem such a frightening prospect? Should we not rejoice at the idea that people will be able to produce more and more by working less and less, so that technology finally frees them from the ancient curse laid down in Genesis: 'Thou shalt earn thy bread by the sweat of thy brow'?

No, we should not rejoice. Apart from all the value attached to work as a means of self-fulfilment, socialization, dignity and personal autonomy, the basic problem for the organization of the economy is still that of individual or collective *solvency*, which is an inescapable consequence in any exchange economy subjected to resource scarcity. In a market economy where hardly anything exists other than individual buyers, the traditional institutional solution is evidently that of individual solvency.

This has not fundamentally changed today, and the old curse persists precisely in the prevailing institutional rules. To be sure, the productive apparatuses are now capable of producing more with less human effort. But remuneration of the factors of production remains the basic instrument governing access to the wealth produced, and the immense majority of men and women own no factor of production other than their own labour-power. Thus each individual's paid labour, or each household's paid labour, is still the chief means of insertion into the activity of the community – not only for the purposes of production, but also for the elementary consumption essential to each individual's survival.

This situation is by no means decreed by fate, and we must clearly understand its *institutional* character. It is time we saw the difficulties arising today as the result not of some divine malediction but of people's inability to organize their own collective life. A number of factors come into play here.

We are considering a situation that has to do with economics; the necessity for distribution and arbitration arises from the scarcity of means in relation to the needs that have to be satisfied. But we should first recall that the indefinite creation of limitless needs is itself a human invention; and above all that private property, along with the market, is one of the basic institutions of our society, applying in particular to the factors of production themselves. Thus, for the satisfaction of even their most basic needs, most people do not have much to offer for exchange on the market other than their own labour-power – primarily, though not exclusively, by means of paid work.

We must also ask why technological change generally favours capital-intensive factor combinations, or at least combinations with a low intensity of unskilled labour. This is the kind of question to which Karl Marx tried to give a comprehensive answer for his own epoch. Some circumstances have changed since then, of course, but not all – and certainly not the basic logic of the system. We desperately lack an analysis of sufficient profundity and complexity to renew the Marxist interpretation, but one must be sought in the institutional conditions for the accumulation of profit.

Indefinite creation of needs (including the most artificial ones), sanctification of private property, a tendency to the generalization of commodity exchange and wage labour: these are the crucial characteristics of contemporary capitalist society and its accelerated globalization. With many adjustments to compensate for them? No doubt. The richest countries, at least, have varying degrees of redistributive taxation, social protection, unemployment insurance, public services, and so on. Yet these very adjustments are now being wound down in the majority of countries, for no other reason than the advance of marketization itself, the accumulation of profit and the reduced role of the state (with budget deficits as the main pretext).

The evil goes deeper still. For, as Karl Polanyi already noted,[4] the commodification of human labour is one of the most shocking elements in the general expansion of the realm of the commodity. Whereas the nature of the commodity is precisely to be an anonymous *thing* that can be alienated and exchanged for other things, labour is closely bound up with a unique *person*: it is part of their identity, the mark of their insertion into nature and human society. From this point of view, few terms in the present-day vocabulary of economics are as unacceptable – because based upon a wholly illegitimate amalgam – as 'human capital' or 'human resources'. But who takes exception to them nowadays?

As a result of these simultaneous trends (simultaneous because they stem from the same systemic logic), we find with some surprise – unless we happen to be an orthodox economist – that the economy has less and less need of human beings.[5] Hence the solutions of the past become inadequate, and new discourses make their appearance. But perhaps these are no more than discourses.

The old 'Fordist' recipe is obsolete. Henry Ford once saw that he would have to pay his workers more so that they could buy the cars they produced. But two major things have happened since then. First, what is called 'technological progress' has been replacing workers with robots. This would be cause for rejoicing if the goods produced for consumption were distributed in accordance with the priority needs of the whole population. But the strict rules of consumer solvency have not changed – above all, the imperative that, leaving aside some (dwindling) measures of redistribution, one must have participated in production, either through labour or through capital, in order to participate in the distribution of income, and therefore in consumption.

Faced with this contradiction, the people in charge react first of all by clinging, in the most general terms, to the old discourse: restore overall *growth* as the priority, and the jobs will come as well. Yet the reality is that growth returns only slowly and fitfully; it cannot be expected to regain the long-term rates of the past; the prospect of indefinite growth has to be abandoned as a panacea for the problems of the economy. The immediate reality, moreover, is that short-term growth often destroys more jobs than it creates. In the space of twenty-five years, for example, the world's five hundred leading multinational companies boosted their sales sevenfold, without increasing the total labour force in their employ.[6]

This brings us to the second discourse. To each region or country that finds itself in difficulties because a declining sum of wages and workers means a declining number of consumers, the neoliberal globalization of modernity proposes the myth of *external markets*: you must sell where there is solvent demand; if it does not exist within your own frontiers, you must look for it in export markets. This discourse does not explain that such a solution can be applied only for a temporary period during which some countries are able to export to others which still lack the same productive capacity; or that if the countries which buy the exports have no equivalent to sell in exchange, the process will rapidly grind to a halt as debts rise, and 'restructuring' is imposed in the name of international order. Nor does it explain what will happen after that temporary period is over, appearing simply to believe that the process will continue through the spread of development, since the best partner for a developed country is another developed country.

All this raises numerous questions. The first and most fundamental, which underlines the topicality of the Marxian analysis, concerns the long-term future of a system that accumulates profit through the extraction of surplus-value from labour – when labour itself is diminishing. A more immediate cause for concern, however, is the exclusion and marginalization that have appeared on a massive scale in every society around the world, including the most prosperous.

A new and singularly odd paradox thus hangs over our economic and social system: it is capable of the most extraordinary technological achievements, and therefore of unprecedented growth in output, yet it cannot organize itself in such a way that its own products are available to all members of society. In the short term, then, the growing output is skewed towards a certain kind of consumption by privileged groups, which does not necessarily correspond to the needs that should be recognized as social priorities. In the short term, too, though as yet only on an *ad hoc* basis, numerous phenomena associated with overproduction have been making their appearance – a trend which fuels fierce competition among global firms to expand, or simply to preserve, their 'market shares'. (Cases in point are shipbuilding and automobiles,[7] soon doubtless to be joined by the aeronautical industry, and the ruthless competition among countries and regions to attract international tourism, however great the ecological destruction it involves.) In the longer term, we may well see a return of the oldest spectres of the market economy – general overproduction and falling sales – as well as new threats linked with the final depletion of certain non-renewable natural resources, or with an irreversible change in such components of the ecosystem as climate or biodiversity.

These dangers are too clear, and too grave, for the societies affected by the crisis of work to remain totally passive. In any case, they are not remaining passive. The debate is already developing into a search for various kinds of solution. What type of future do they indicate?

THE FUTURE OF WORK AND EMPLOYMENT

The question of employment is today at the heart of economic policy debates in most industrial countries. It is also on the agenda in developing countries, of course: it is not always formulated there in the same terms, since wage-earners do not yet make up as high a proportion of the total population,[8] but it is an essential part of strategies to combat poverty and raise living standards.

It should be stressed again that these are highly complex questions, and so far no one has been able to come up with satisfactory answers to them. The most solidly based work in this field has shown how apparently rational and well-intentioned proposals can have negative effects that no one wished.[9] Thus, when there is a greater need than ever for intellectual rigour, it would be presumptuous for us to claim to be offering original solutions, or even a deeper re-examination of fairly sophisticated technical debates that now fill whole bookcases. As I have said on other matters, my aim here is only to present the possible solutions to the problem of work in the light of the overall system of capitalist modernity and its underlying pursuit of profit.

We have just recalled that, even if there is a certain reluctance to consider human labour as one commodity among others, its use in practice as a factor of production subjects it to the demands of economic rationality. We have also seen that labour, and especially work for a wage, is for most people their only means of access to consumption of the goods and services produced in society, since the possibility of consuming them depends upon effective demand. However, the criteria for rational use of labour as a factor by entrepreneurs – criteria associated with more or less long-term maximization of profit – do not in all cases fit in with people's need for work to gain access to consumption. The crucial difficulty appears when, for reasons to do with technological innovation and the relative prices of the factors of production, manufacturers (who by definition think micro-economically) have 'less and less need of human labour', because they can replace it more profitably with other factors of production.

This explains the importance attached to the *macro*-economic question of market outlets, and the initial postulate that solutions are to be found only in a revival of aggregate growth and a sharper external reorientation of the economy. But the patent inadequacy of such solutions has led to more and more proposals for a new orientation, ranging from the adoption of more labour-intensive technologies to the administrative regulation of employment and incomes; from an increase in public service jobs to a sharing out of work time; from a guaranteed minimum income to the development of a 'third sector' geared to a huge layer of socially important needs that are neglected by the market economy. Present difficulties – in France, especially those concerning the introduction of a 35-hour week – suggest that the various solutions envisaged for the future are all incomplete, and that they will therefore need to complement rather than compete with one another.

These difficulties, it must be said, are tending to discourage large numbers of officials and observers, as well as to spread doubts about whether 'full employment' is still a realistic aim for our societies. They also pose the question of whether the right to basic consumption should not be much more radically separated from participation in commodity production.

How are we to make progress on these complex issues? The aim of our reflections here cannot be to discuss in technical detail various solutions that might be conceived. But since these reflections are meant to address the totality of the problem, it may be in order to begin by making two points.

First, at the level of principle, we can discuss whether demands for 'full employment' in the traditional sense of the term are still 'realistic' in the present context of the world economy. The answer to this probably has to be no. But, on the other hand, there can be no questioning the legitimacy of the demand that all members of a community should be able to remain alive, in decent conditions of existence. In this sense, the economic debate cannot be dissociated from its ethical dimension, and more broadly from its implications for the promotion and respect of 'human rights'.

Second, it is important to remind ourselves of the role that can be played by human institutions. As we have seen, the system of capitalist modernity eventually commodifies human labour itself, which becomes the object of market supply and demand just like any other product or material. But over and above any ethical objections on principle to this process of commodification, we must again consider the practical functioning of the market. The fact that exchange is market exchange does not mean that relationships of forces can freely express themselves and assert themselves in their natural state, nor that they are inviolable in the name of some abstract logic. On the contrary, institutional rules and restrictions frame the operation of the market in ways that vary from society to society, defining what is and is not accepted as exchange, what is and is not recognized as a valid way of setting prices, and hence the rights and duties of all trading partners. It is precisely this institutional component subject to human decision which seems to be neglected by those who insist on respect for market 'equilibria' in relation to work.

Jacques Lesourne argues these points in exemplary fashion.[10] He showed long ago that no market functions entirely satisfactorily; that labour markets are far from being perfectly competitive, and must be analysed in terms of the 'social oligopoly' (that is, the unequal relations of power between groups within society) specific to a given time and place. He is certainly not unaware of the institutional dimensions, and shows that they can be modified only at a sluggish pace, and probably only by technocratic means. He is also unquestionably right to insist that, while the theoretical explanations of unemployment differ in many ways (Keynesian conceptions being diametrically opposed to structural or classical theories), reality mixes them all together and makes it very hard to chart a coherent line of political action. Nevertheless, Lesourne does propose a kind of sanctification of the market as a way of expressing needs, and therefore as the *only* criterion for the evaluation of needs and the protection of the famous economic 'equilibria', with the inevitable requirements of growth and profitability.

This systematic bias in favour of the logic of the market appear to me a rigid barrier that needs to be overcome, even if it is not yet clear how this might be achieved. At least the negative critique developed above may indicate some positive principles to guide reflection and research.

- Questions relating to work and employment involve human aspects (dignity, the right to life, the right to social integration, etc.) that go well beyond the logic of purely economic rationalization. Any approach that limits itself to economics is therefore inadequate; no economic reasoning, however rigorous, can be the sole basis for a solution to these problems.

- Economic reasoning remains essential, of course, but an attempt must be made to ground it on an approach broader than mere market rationalization, in the sense explained at length in previous chapters. Work is an individual issue, but it is also a collective issue. As such, it depends on the decision not only of market actors but also of the community at large. This has at least two implications. First of all, it is up to the community to define – through an explicit assessment of social priorities – the *institutional framework* within which problems of work, including the labour market, will be resolved: for example, the maximum number of working hours, health and safety requirements, restrictions on the labour of children or a particular social group, or the right to universal benefits. Through various regulations, however, and within the room for manoeuvre created by the interchangeability of factors of production, this institutional framework may also define the operational conditions for the distribution of value-added between capital and labour, or between the various categories of labour. This distribution, which is at the centre of the political problems of work and employment, does not depend exclusively (as many have claimed it does) on an abstract and inviolable logic of market rationalization.

The argument may be carried further, even if the economists' 'official' theoretical apparatus does not easily lend itself to such purposes. When neoliberal economists observe a price in the market, they think it derives from a relationship between supply and demand that must be protected from 'distortions', perhaps even in the name of the community. But if we agree to go beyond a purely market definition of economic rationality, such a restriction no longer has any reason for existence. Why not accept that the interest expressed by the community should be added to the overall demand of individual market actors? (This will distort competition among the various actors, of course, but this happens anyway in actually existing markets.) In terms of work and employment, this means that public demand would play a dual role: it would *substitute itself* for market demand when that is failing, and claim a certain quantity of labour for tasks that are considered 'socially useful' (even if they escape the rationality of the market); and it would *supplement* market demand to form aggregate demand, thereby modifying the 'equilibrium' quantity and price on the labour market in such a way that no higher logic would be able to detect any 'distortion' in this. It might be objected that such theoretical subtlety has no practical effect on all the concrete questions of macroeconomic management. But nothing is less certain. For at least the mixed economy would be given an acceptable rationalization in the eyes of economists, and therefore an intellectual legitimacy that would make it safe from the misguided encroachment of purely market interests. Obviously, however, such a theory still has to be constructed, and then coherently inserted into an enlarged economic theory.

CONCLUSION:
PLURALISM AND SOLVENCY

This cursory glance at the future of work and employment may now be concluded with two observations. One concerns an inevitable conflict with mainstream thinking in this field; the other refers to the solvency requirement.

As a specialist in economic projection, Jacques Lesourne opens the concluding two chapters of his work with the following statement: 'For us human beings ... the future is by nature plural; it is produced by a mixture of necessity, chance and volition.'[11] We can only agree that *the future of work will necessarily be plural* – that is, marked by complexity; no panacea can be glimpsed that would solve all the problems. This is a conclusion shared by most 'serious' experts and decision-makers in the field, and it seems to command acceptance more than ever before.

One characteristic of all currently proposed solutions to the problem of work explains, however, why it seems so difficult for them to gain acceptance: they are all opposed, in one way or another, to the logic of capitalist modernity and its neoliberal globalization, which claims to know no other criterion for decisions than indefinite accumulation of the maximum profit. The future of work is thus one of the most essential problems of our societies – both because of the human issues involved, and because of the obstacle that it inevitably runs up against in the logic of the system itself. Solutions will remain mere 'tinkering' so long as they fail to distance themselves from that logic – so long as political reflection, debate and action fail to recognize that we live in societies too complex for regulation by a single criterion, even such a fundamental one as individual interest and the accumulation of profit.

My second concluding point is to recall the general principle already mentioned in connection with the expression of needs and the necessity of arbitrating between them. Whatever its origin, scarcity (absolute or relative) entails an obligation to choose. In a market economy, such choice is guided by the encounter between solvent demand and the pursuit of profit. In a collectivist economy, a decision may be made to disregard the criterion of individual solvency, but society as a whole still has to be solvent – for its choices make sense only if they are supported by the collective supply of necessary resources. The same requirement applies if all citizens, whether in paid employment or not, are to be assured a minimum level of consumption or a 'universal benefit'. Society has to express a 'solvent collective demand' by offering to allocate the necessary resources, and therefore to withhold them from other possible uses.

This principle, which seems elementary enough, raises a difficult problem of calculation. How can we tell whether there is 'solvent collective demand' for the building of a new opera house, except by way of an always debatable reference to the public will as expressed by an authority whose legitimacy is beyond debate? How can the urgency of this demand be compared with that of other collective needs? Such dilemmas are enough to make one regret the usefulness of a market system of prices!

Moreover, these are not just problems of calculation; they involve choices about social goals. This is why there has to be the greatest possible clarity about the question of work. If the ultimate aim of economic and social organization remains the maximization of growth, the most intensive exploitation of natural resources, the indefinite boosting of national strength, or the accumulation of profit by those who make the decisions, then there is simply no room left for a genuine policy on work. But if the priority of society is clearly stated to be the

right of all to life and self-fulfilment, as well as respect for human
beings and their creativity, then a policy on work becomes possible
even in the context of a widespread market economy – although it will
be able to take shape only if the capitalist logic is so profoundly
modified that it no longer seeks to base the social system upon a single
criterion.

CHAPTER 9

THE CONTRADICTIONS
OF GLOBALIZATION

I would define 'globalization' as freedom for my company to invest where it wants for as long as it wants, and to produce whatever it wants, by getting its supplies and selling its products wherever it wants, and by having to endure the fewest possible constraints in labour law and collective agreements.

President of the Swiss–Swedish group ABB in 1995
(quoted by François Chesnais in 'Observatoire de la
mondialisation', *Lumière sur l'AMI*, 1998, p. 19)

It may seem unnecessary to add a chapter on 'globalization' to this brief analysis of the contradictions and impasses of modernity, whose worldwide expansionist thrust has been repeatedly discussed throughout. If globalization is understood as an acceleration and intensification of exchanges among various players within the expanding system of modernity, then it is evidently a process which cannot but sharpen the contradictions and worsen the blockages that we have already identified at sub-global levels.

Nevertheless, this globalization process brings new players onto the scene, and transforms the relationship of forces among those present on it. By sharpening the contradictions and raising them to a higher level of generality, it also enables us to understand better some of their forms, and makes some of their consequences more profound. Since the whole set of relationships that we observe is ever more clearly dominated by this global dimension, it would be rather careless on our part not to try to draw out its main implications.

In this chapter, we shall therefore briefly look, first, at the changing relations among various players and their consequences in terms of dependence or domination, inequality or exclusion, as well as of regulation of the world economy; second, at what accelerated liberalization implies for the general interest in these international exchanges; and third, at some specific effects of such liberalization in the area of agricultural trade. Once again, our aim will be to suggest a number of contradictions through analysis of the underlying systemic logics, rather than to present an exhaustive picture of the whole or even a detailed account of a particular set of phenomena.

THE EMERGENCE OF NEW PLAYERS AND THE HEIGHTENING OF TENSIONS WITHIN THE SYSTEM

Globalization may be understood as a process that changes the sites and levels of economic decision-making, or at least some of them.[1] Most recent analyses of globalization share a threefold emphasis on the players within the world economy:

- First, power in the market economy is concentrated to a fantastic extent in a small number of 'multinational' or 'transnational' corporations and their national branches. Of course, this concentration does not do away with the millions of smaller firms and individual production units, still less with the millions or billions of other producers, intermediaries and consumers active in the world economy. But it does profoundly alter, in favour of the big corporations, the relative strength of these various players, both in terms of resources and in their exchange of commodities, services, production factors, and especially labour.

- A small number of international public organizations emerge at both global and regional levels. The states which have jointly created these organizations have given them often quite considerable legislative, regulatory and financial powers, which also serve to alter the relationship of forces in economic decisions. Think, for example, of the gradual removal of non-tariff barriers and the new rules governing competition in international trade, or the international norms proclaimed in matters of health, or the conditions attached to public or even private international loans.

- There has consequently been a significant change in the place and role of national public authorities (a role we shall examine more closely in Chapter 10). This change is often analysed as a unilateral reduction in the role of states to the benefit of large transnational corporations or international organizations. But the phenomenon is doubtless more complex, as we shall see, and it requires further analysis of the new types of relationship that are – or ought to be – established between public sector and market economy.

These new power relations – like the equivocal phenomenon of globalization in general (myth or reality? ideology or irreversible historical reality?) – will not be the object of analysis in this chapter. As before, we shall merely draw out certain characteristics of the system and some of its typical relations, with a view to offering an overall interpretation. But this precisely raises the question of which characteristics of the system are of greatest significance for the process of globalization.

Some of these are evident enough, but they need to be recalled if we are to focus on their less evident implications in other fields. As the global pretensions of modernity become more pronounced, it continues to be a social system preoccupied with economics – and an economics essentially grounded upon the postulates of *market* economy. Without repeating everything that has been said before, we may note that this evolution accentuates the impersonal, anonymous character of the social relations established by the system, especially as its expansionist thrust exerts a pressure towards uniformity in social behaviour (consumption patterns, lifestyles, reference values, career ambitions, criteria for social advancement) which downgrades such opposing values as mutual support, disinterested friendliness, or even self-affirmation and individual goals in life.

The world economic system – which will form a kind of obligatory frame of reference for individual and group behaviour – and the emerging world social system should be analysed, in the manner of market economy itself, as a juxtaposition of *rival* interests and players whose exchanges with one another are governed mainly by the market criteria of solvent demand and profit accumulation. The 'collective expression' of these individual interests, if we may put it like that, will be limited to quantifiable macroeconomic aggregates (consumption, savings, investment, debt, exports, inflation, employment, unemployment, growth, budget deficits, and so on). It will say very little about social objectives, community goals, or non-monetary relations between individuals, families and groups; it will scarcely heed the ways in which people live together; and it will be silent about the meaning that social organization should have if people are to live in peace around the world, with a minimum of satisfaction that is not reducible to market consumption, ownership of objects or accumulation of profit.

The poverty of social relations in modernity has already been discussed. But the currently unthinking, even compulsory, mode of reference to a huge and abstract entity called 'the world economy' – as if it were a natural or social entity that needed no further explanation – will itself aggravate the abstract, seemingly disembodied character of that economy, its remoteness from the most immediate or essential needs of men and women. It also tends to conceal the real issues that preoccupy the new players dominating the world economy, and hence to accentuate the inequality of power and results, and the relations of dependence within a system which, though it is tremendously productive, is even less capable than before of solving some of the most elementary and pressing problems of humanity. Let us pause for a moment on these points.

The unequal power of decision-making is an obvious fact. What remains of the 'consumer sovereignty' so dear to market theory, when the global productive system draws no longer just on the technostructure of a 'New Industrial State' (exposed by Galbraith more than thirty years ago in relation to the US economy[2]) but upon the strengthened hegemony of the United States itself, and the power of huge global corporations? What is left even of individual liberty, that ideological pretext constantly evoked by the masters of the system, when the global financial markets exercise the most abstract of all dictatorships? What remains of national economic sovereignty (with or without planners), when the international division of labour more and more signifies for the 'developing countries' a monopolistic exploitation of their natural resources for the benefit of a minority of the world's population? What remains of the power of local communities to safeguard their autonomy and their supplies, in the face of a global economy that is supposedly decentralized according to the principle of market competition, but in reality more and more centralized because the productive system is increasingly 'oligopolistic' (that is, dependent upon a small number of corporations)? What is the meaning of the 'recommendations' (more often than not, instructions) issued 'in the interests of the world economy and global equilibrium' to national politicians and officials by international organizations such as the IMF, WTO or World Bank (and, to a lesser extent, various UN agencies or even the G7), when it can be shown that the same world economy is firmly geared to a few interests whose power is totally out of proportion to the number of people they represent?

The results of this unequal power of decision are not slow to show up in an unequal distribution of the total product and income, or quite simply in unequal access to resources. Hence the frightening, but hardly disputable, estimates of international organizations about the growth of world poverty and the spread of colossal inequalities among social groups. With regard to the UNDP social indicators in Chapter 2, two points will appear even more clearly in this context of economic globalization.

First, there is a hugely increased sense of alienation among the people affected by such poverty and imbalances, as the responsibility for them seems to lie completely outside their control, and they feel like victims of a vast global machinery whose momentum is said to be irreversible and which no one can affect in any way. We shall return to this fundamental lack of responsibility in the system of modernity. But the global economy is also incapable of really addressing the problems of inequality and mounting a genuine 'war on poverty' – ultimately because, in the prevailing system of market economy, the role of national and international public authorities must be kept within a neoliberal straitjacket serving the interests of the market and its dominant players. Since the nineteenth century, social constraints have forced national capitalisms to apply various corrections to the free market, but these corrections are still of only minor importance in the globalized capitalism of the late twentieth and early twenty-first centuries. 'Development aid', in particular, is quite marginal in comparison with the scale of international financial flows, and, in any case, the correction of social imbalances is hardly one of its main purposes. The 'war on poverty' remains an unconvincing incantation, in so far as the structural and systemic roots of poverty are not even mentioned by those who claim to be waging this 'war'. And, as we shall see, the most 'protective' measures in recent international legislation actually protect the interests of the strongest rather than the weakest.

We can now understand better the huge obstacles in the way of 'social development' – all the more numerous when we pass from the national level to the global level (which certainly cannot be ignored). What is at issue is not only inequality, poverty, marginalization or even temporary exclusion of a considerable part of the world's population, in the South but also in the North; we have to ask ourselves, more radically and more dramatically, whether this is not becoming a definitive, irreversible exclusion from 'development' – not from any kind of development, of course (here lies the real reason for hope), but from the kind presently spread by the global system.

If this proves to be the case, we would have to look very differently at 'the imperatives of globalization' and 'the interests of the global economy', which in fact are the interests of a privileged minority. We can understand why that minority defends its privileges, but we cannot accept its false claim to be the vanguard of a social progress that will soon be shared by all. The analysis of inequality and exclusion thus powerfully reinforces the main argument of this book: that today's global system of development cannot be generalized; that a different kind of development must be set for the world economy if it is claimed to be in the service of all.

The arguments concerning economic growth that will be presented here in relation to free trade, protectionism and structural adjustment point in the same direction.

FREE TRADE AND GROWTH

The system of modernity encourages free trade at an international level. This is so not only because the system is based on market economics – particularly on free initiative, competition and private appropriation – and because the inspiration behind it is individualist and neoliberal, but also because this perspective is supposed to provide the most 'effective' mechanisms of resource allocation within an international division of labour theoretically grounded upon comparative advantages. Here, of course, effectiveness is understood in the sense of yielding not the best possible response to the needs expressed, but the greatest possible level of profit, commodity output and monetary income.

This simple reminder hardly requires further explanation. But some of its implications deserve to be considered at greater length, so sharply do they conflict with the appearance of common sense that one is tempted to see in them. We shall therefore now focus on the discrepancies between the practice of free trade and the theoretical justifications of it, before briefly evoking the specific problems linked with food and agriculture.

What, nowadays, is understood by *freedom* of trade? It should be taken in a fundamentally negative sense, as the rejection of any constraints and the prohibition of any measure that might 'distort' the competitive situation among individual candidates for the role of trading partner. This conception is in turn based upon three postulates: that the market mechanism is the best suited to achieve the general interest, through the free pursuit of particular interests; that trade (including international trade) plays a positive role in promoting growth, and therefore the general welfare; and that the international trading markets do in fact come close to a situation of perfect competition.

We shall not dwell here on the first and most general of these postulates, as we shall anyway have to return to the notion of a general interest and the actual components of 'development'. The second argument, initially formulated in terms of growth in general, accepts that it is necessary to take into account a number of variables (the most evident being the dimension of the national economy, since smaller economies are naturally under greater pressure to open up), but then lays down a positive correlation between the degree of openness to commercial and financial exchange and the medium-term rate of economic growth.

This correlation cannot be regarded as firmly established, precisely because it involves a considerable number of variables, and the existing statistical evidence (especially that assembled by the World Bank and its consultants) is not beyond dispute. Furthermore, the argument runs up against the fundamental critique outlined above concerning the adequacy of growth as a general criterion of development, and about its applicability to every type of country, whatever its level of income. For the correlation between free trade and growth appears especially vulnerable if it is the case that free trade is ultimately of benefit only to the richest and most powerful.

Nor is this all. The postulate concerning the beneficial character of international trade makes a general principle out of the opening of economies and societies to all kinds of external exchange (commercial, financial, cultural, and so on – the implicit exception being migration); it sets maximum openness as a necessary condition for the maximization of welfare or the general interest, for all members of these economies and societies. Let us try once more to avoid being simplistic. It must be accepted, of course, that an economy open to outside ideas, values, products and technologies has much greater potential than an autarkic, closed economy. The choice is not between total openness and total closure; the real question is *how great the openness should be, and in whose favour*. It is here that ideology – that is, implicit political choices – come into play. Neoliberal globalizers assert the categorical imperative of maximum openness to every kind of international exchange, on the grounds that the resulting economic efficiency is supposedly to the advantage of all. In most cases, therefore, they rule out any protection of the weakest interests in society. Yet we now know that his correlation between maximum openness and general interest stems from an abstract, timeless assertion, which does not take account of the legitimate preferences and adjustment difficulties of people living in the real world. Numerous historical experiences fail to bear it out, and a number of recent events (from layoffs on grounds of international competitiveness in Europe to the consequences of structural adjustment in the countries of the South) demonstrate the utterly illusory character of this 'general interest' linked to maximum openness.

The third of the postulates listed above – which claims to find the competition of economic theory present in the reality of international trade – is certainly the easiest to disprove today in the light of experience. Paul Bairoch, for example, has forcefully shown that throughout history the doctrine of free trade has been evoked only by those in a position of international strength, and to serve their own interests.[3] The growing inequality of power, which we have just described in relation to the accelerated globalization of the last two decades, evidently increases the distance between the actual conditions obtaining on world markets and the schema of perfect competition. The multilateral organizations that have concerned themselves with the management of international commercial and financial exchanges have obviously not been ignorant of this situation; we can find traces of their awareness of it in a series of international regulations governing which states are allowed to take measures to protect or 'safeguard' certain national interests (balance-of-payments equilibrium, security factors, even cultural policy,[4]) or the particular interests of some of their nationals facing international competition.

The first thing to note, however, is that these theoretical exceptions are extremely modest in scope: very few collective interests seem to merit protection in the eyes of these international censors, whether it is a question of the products of fledgling industries (who remembers the arguments of Friedrich List?), products representing a particular cultural tradition, the prerequisites of food autonomy, or *a fortiori* the arms trade. On the other hand, one of the most blatantly protectionist elements in recent international negotiations (the Uruguay Round, which led to the creation of the World Trade Organization in 1993) concerned trade-related intellectual property measures (TRIPs), and it essentially protected Western patent-holders. Also worth noting here is the considerable discrepancy between what the dominant players do themselves (the liberties they can take because of their power) and what they allow the dominated players to do.

To be quite blunt, the countries which control global exchanges preach ultra-free trade and succeed in imposing it relatively strictly on the weakest countries, yet practise escalating protectionism with one another. The recent history of relations among the three partners of the 'Triad' (United States, European Union, Japan) is a perfect case in point.

The history so far of GATT and the WTO – institutions whose desirability cannot be disputed in principle – is not a very convincing defence of the interests of the huge majority of the world's population. But it is necessary to understand the reasons for this, which lie deeper than the twists and turns of current negotiations. Once again, these reasons are linked to the fundamental logic of the global system itself. The WTO wants to generalize the market principle to the totality of human international relations: everything is a commodity in its eyes; every exchange belongs in the domain of trade, and is therefore subject to the rules of competition, which exclude all other rules. Hence the attempt to substitute the rules of commercial law for all other rules, including those associated with human rights.[5] Hence, too, the awesome speed with which the indefinite extension of ultra-liberal globalization and a falling back on national sovereignty have come to be presented as polar opposites in recent international debate, whereas the really crucial question concerns the new ways that have to be invented of *selectively* inserting each national community into a global society still to be built.[6]

Beyond the objective diversity of the interests in play, it was the (still embryonic) awareness of this diversity – and, more broadly, of the profoundly ambivalent relationship between world trade and social progress – which caused the failure of the Seattle meeting in December 1999 to get a new round of international negotiations under way. But many signs of the general difficulties in international relations had appeared long before the breakdown in Seattle. For example, attempts to introduce a 'social clause' into world trade (to prevent various abuses, especially distortions of competition, linked to children's and prisoners' labour and working conditions considered unacceptable by Western standards) were resisted by developing countries for reasons of 'sovereignty' or 'comparative advantage'. The legitimacy of these arguments varied quite considerably, but at least some of them rightly charged the richer countries with practising a form of disguised protectionism. Moreover, following the crises in Africa, Kosovo and Indonesia, a wider debate has emerged over the legitimacy of humanitarian or other international involvement – a debate which, though heavily skewed by historical responsibilities, by the unequal relationship of forces, and by hidden agendas on one side or the other, cannot be postponed indefinitely. It will be necessary to clarify the basic facts and principles at stake, and to move towards the adoption of new international rules in this domain.

But let us return to strictly economic exchanges. It can be confidently asserted that, on the seemingly honourable pretexts of economic efficiency and social justice, the debate over free trade or protectionism has become a major area of confusion, where the most legitimate arguments jostle the most indefensible hypocrisy. Here, certainly, there can be no defending the blind references to 'theory', and to the supposed inevitability of the logic underlying the system.

Nevertheless, the debate remains at much too general a level to allow a clear-cut conclusion to be drawn about specific problems. Nor is this the kind of conclusion intended here, since our aim is only to identify the main questions relating to development that can be raised in the face of the one-dimensional logic of neoliberal modernity. A number of cases particularly reinforce the sense of unease over development, but here we shall limit ourselves to that of food and agriculture.

THE EXAMPLE OF FOOD AND AGRICULTURE

If there is one incontestable 'basic human need', it must be for the food that gives people the means to life and health – and to a certain security in this respect. This elementary observation should be borne in mind when we examine the arguments in favour of free trade, especially those which focus on growth and maintain that perfect competition results in a social optimum.

It is undeniable that trading possibilities, especially at an international level, create a powerful incentive to increase the production of agricultural commodities; it is also highly likely that involvement in trade actually does increase total production. One of the most significant historical examples of such a correlation is the experience of the European Union, although we should remember that this involved not only openness to trade but also a veritable 'common agricultural policy' and powerful budgetary instruments. The results have certainly exceeded all expectations, so that now it has become necessary to combat the effects of overproduction. But those results cannot just be reproduced in any context: not only because the availability of production factors is obviously not the same, but also because the index of success in Europe has been total exportable production, whereas elsewhere exports have to compete with large-scale internal demand, which, solvent or not, is a matter of survival for the populations concerned.

Now, this kind of use rivalry is a characteristic feature of the less privileged countries, where farmland is not always available in sufficient quantity to feed the whole indigenous population, and where the greater 'profitability' of exports, and – even more – the inflow of cheaper imports, may be serious obstacles to production for internal consumption. This situation is exacerbated – as we shall see in a moment – by the unequal character of the competition.

Thus, although a country's aggregate production may well rise through an opening to international trade, the *structure* of that production will reflect the structure of solvent demand in external markets rather than the structure of internal needs, and imports may threaten the very viability of certain types of production inside the country. Generally speaking, the new structure of production will have no chance of reflecting the structure of the most pressing needs when these cannot find expression in solvent demand. The increase in output attributable to an opening of the economy will be an increase in market output under the constraints of profitability; it will in principle not be concerned with any social benefits linked to greater availability of agricultural products, still less with any social costs not expressed in market calculations. The key players will simply not take into account the costs of increased output in terms of soil exhaustion, reduced biodiversity and difficulties in renewing natural resources (including forest), or in terms of 'collateral damage' caused by the use of 'genetically modified strains', as well as many other consequences not subject to market calculation.

Especially in the non-industrialized countries, the opening of agriculture to free trade will therefore tend to increase export production but not necessarily production for local use. The dominant interests will certainly favour this trend: first, because it goes together with higher levels of debt and structural adjustment programmes designed to raise the foreign currency for debt repayment; and second, because the principal players in the export sector enjoy a privileged position that we should now briefly describe.

Agricultural markets, particularly those linked to export, can scarcely be considered as perfectly competitive markets. This is due not to the involvement of large numbers of small individual producers, but to the fact that the conditions of supply, demand and exchange are controlled by a small number of transnational corporations, whose aim in life is the accumulation of power and profit for themselves much more than the meeting of local needs that might be essential for certain groups in society. Far from achieving the optimum proclaimed by mainstream theory, the operation of this type of market leads to a *cumulative strengthening of inequalities*: unequal access to the factors of production (especially land, but also managerial skills and inputs affording a short-term rise in productivity); unequal remuneration (reinforced by imperfect competition all along the chain of middlemen); and unequal decision-making power (expressed in unequal satisfaction of needs for the various players).

CONCLUSION

The current protests against agricultural liberalization measures decided in the framework of the WTO – protests driven especially by poorer farmers, both in Europe and in the so-called developing countries – may readily be understood as an attack on the whole range of aberrations inherent in the logic of the dominant system. These aberrations, highlighted by the quickening pace of globalization, may be summed up in the following picture, which is unfortunately by no means a caricature.

- Defenders of the dominant system claim that the mechanisms of market competition (solvent demand and the accumulation of profit) promote the general interest both by maximizing aggregate output and by allocating it to the most pressing needs.
- In reality, this increase in aggregate output leads to overproduction (because the growth in agricultural supply is geared to those who need it least), and the overproduction is then sanctioned through reduced purchase prices especially for the producers of primary materials.[7] But this increased output also means that certain essential needs (the needs of those who cannot afford to pay) are not satisfied, because the system is not concerned about whether aggregate production matches the structure of real needs. Of course, these real needs are not necessarily reflected in solvent demand at prevailing prices, especially if internal demand has to compete with the external market (as it actually has to do, for reasons mainly linked with a level of external debt from which the rural world is most unlikely to have benefited). This hiatus between real needs and market supply confirms the basic insight of Amartya Sen: that famines are usually due not to an inadequate supply of food but to the fact that the rules of the market inadequately distribute access to the aggregate food product.[8]
- An aggravating factor is that the overall growth in output is itself achieved at considerable social cost for the world economy as a whole, because it disregards all the costs that fail to enter into the system of international prices. First, there are the environmental costs and those resulting from degradation or exhaustion of the supply of natural resources, which reduce the planet's carrying capacity; but there are also the social imbalances (insecurity, exploitation of the weakest by the strongest, eviction of farmers from their land, rural

depopulation, all the varied forms of exclusion and poverty), which have predictable consequences in terms of violence, unacceptable injustice or, more prosaically, a lack of the public order necessary for the functioning of a market economy. In anything more than a short-term perspective, who can benefit from such havoc?

• In view of these social costs, and in the absence of a political will for fundamental changes in the system, one might think that the various parties would at least agree on some essential points, beginning with the right of every person and every family to decent living conditions, and the right of future generations to inherit a planet that has not been plundered for immediate profit. Such agreement, if reached, would have meant official *protection* of certain rights in the name of higher concerns, and therefore voluntary limits on the freedom of international trade. With ever rarer exceptions, however, it is just such limits which have been fiercely rejected – in the name of liberalism, anti-protectionism and wholehearted free trade – by the interests dominating recent trade negotiations. And this is likely to remain the case – unless the recent failure in Seattle marks the modest beginnings of a new expression of interests diverging from those of the masters of international trade.

Agriculture is, to be sure, not the only example of the ravages of neoliberal globalization, and the analysis should be extended to industry, services, health, education, cultural production and many other spheres, as well as to the various measures designed to strengthen the freedom of international investors in any field. But the internationalization of agriculture, and its 'liberalization' in the sense of an extraordinarily restrictive concept of liberty that ultimately comes down to freedom of enterprise and profit-making for a tiny minority, constitute a particularly significant example (if only in terms of the number of people affected) of the *degeneration* of modernity. This degeneration, as we have stressed before, is due to the way in which the system uses the accumulation of profit as an instrument of power and the only criterion of decision-making, although that criterion has become much too narrow to regulate a world as complex as ours by itself. A criterion resting upon a narrow and limited rationality thus results in a threefold aberration, at once economic, social and ecological.

CHAPTER 10

THE ROLE OF
PUBLIC AUTHORITIES

Perhaps the most striking characteristic of the end of the twentieth century is the tension between this accelerating process of globalization and the inability of both public institutions and the collective behaviour of human beings to come to terms with it.

The Crisis Decades ... revealed that human collective institutions had lost control over the collective consequences of human action. Indeed, one of the intellectual attractions which helps to explain the brief vogue for the neoliberal utopia was precisely that it purported to by-pass collective human decisions.

Eric Hobsbawm, *The Age of Extremes*, pp. 15, 565.

Following on from growth, inequality, work and international trade, I will take the role of public authorities as the fifth and last example of the consequences of modernity and its neoliberal globalization. And since this theme is inseparable from the redefinition of the general interest, it will provide a transition to the question of political debate that will be taken up in the final part of this work.

The text will refer mainly to the present contradictions in the functioning of the national state that stem from modernity and globalization. But the question is actually wider in scope, affecting all public authorities at global, regional, national and local levels. The treatment of these contradictions will therefore be organized as follows: first, we shall try to show the intrinsic difficulty of defining the role of public authorities in a liberal (and *a fortiori* neoliberal) economy, to assess the rejection of collective institutions which develops as a result, and to examine the problem of rationalizing the role of public authorities when it is not possible to rely upon market-based economic calculation; next we shall identify the practical consequences of the subordinate status that the state is meant to have in relation to market mechanisms. Positive proposals for a new way of approaching this set of problems will then be discussed in the final part of this work.

As in previous chapters, the aim will be to locate the systemic effects of the development of modernity upon the functioning of our societies – in this case, upon the principles governing the present and the desirable role of public authorities, rather than the detailed ways in which that role is or might be discharged. Discussions of what is desirable traditionally run up against the difficulty of defining the general or public interest, but in the context of neoliberal globalization this difficulty is all the greater owing to the new diversity of interests, and of the corresponding levels of decision-making. A number of quite specific questions are raised. For example, does the 'national interest' coincide with the interests of wage-earners, shareholders or consumers – or with all of these at once? Which of them should take priority? Are the existing sectors of activity all equally important from the point of view of the general interest?

AN IDEOLOGY HOSTILE TO
PUBLIC AUTHORITIES

Since modernity rests upon a system of individualist values, it calls into question the role of public authorities in the economy. But globalization, as an acceleration of the move towards modernity, makes this questioning more intense – especially with regard to the role of the national state.

The first and most fundamental reason for this, of course, is that the globalization of modernity is grounded upon neoliberal ideology. The traditional liberal postulate holds that the general interest is best achieved through the free play of particular interests. Neoliberalism takes this further, and maintains that public authorities should have only the minimal economic function of maintaining order and providing some infrastructural services; they should not intervene to promote the general interest, either positively or correctively, since this results spontaneously from the competitive operation of the market. Actual markets may only rarely meet the conditions of pure and perfect competition that ensure optimality, but in the neoliberal view the imperfections of government action are likely to give greater cause for concern than those of the market.

There is a second reason, however, for the questioning of public intervention. As we have seen, the neoliberal evolution of modernity is marked by a further paradox: it increases the number of collective problems and social-ecological imbalances (greater inequality, fewer job opportunities, more severe environmental degradation), but at the same time, on the pretext of not interfering with the play of the market and introducing a different logic, it opposes the emergence and activity of the collective institutions that are needed to address the new problems facing the community. It also opposes, at least in theory, the expansion of 'compulsory levies' (national and local taxes, social security contributions), claiming that they have already gone beyond the psychological and financial limits of tolerance for the individuals and groups in question. We might be tempted to think, however, that the growing sense of unease and disarray in the societies of modernity is not unrelated to the failure to protect collective interests and the resulting solitariness of individual existence, especially for those who have the least and are the least able to fend for themselves.

These risks of global modernity are aggravated by the emergence of new players which are tending to supplant national governments. Some of these are themselves public players (international regulatory bodies such as the WTO, for example), although their division of responsibilities with national public players is not defined by any clear criteria or any clear consensus of views – indeed, voices have been raised to urge that some of them should be quite simply privatized. New players, perhaps the most powerful, have also been appearing within the private economy: 'multinational' or 'transnational' banks and corporations active in the commercial and financial markets, as well as in new technologies. Thus, in the play of the global economy, the dominant interests and players are not necessarily inserted into any one national space, and this simple fact, together with their growing power, is enough for their activities and strategies to escape direct state regulation.

The liberal character of modernity, and its neoliberal accentuation, have further practical implications which are not often seen as such. For this is the context in which economics was born and developed, with the aim of systematically rationalizing human conduct in the face of scarcity. Economics thus became essentially a science of market economy. Of course, economists soon became aware of numerous situations in which the individualist hypotheses of market economics were not borne out, and to deal with this they developed such conceptual tools as the analysis of 'externalities', or the notion of a 'public good', or various aspects of game theory. Nevertheless, market theory kept its dominant position in economics – so much so that work in the 1960s on 'the rationalization of budget choices' (now somewhat forgotten), or more recently on 'new public management',[1] has mainly referred to market theory and its system of prices. There is no reason to suspect the sincerity of that research work, or to downplay its intellectual significance, but the fact remains that one of the deepest and most influential characteristics of neoliberal ideology is its conviction that, in the end, only the 'market approach' to the rationalization of economic behaviour is likely to display the necessary rigour. Any 'collective' or 'non-market' approaches are simply cast into the outer darkness of 'politics' – that is, into the realm of the arbitrary – or else accepted *faute de mieux* as a lesser evil with no possible claim to rigour.

If I dwell on this rationalization of public decisions, it is because it is one of the areas where mainstream economics is at its shakiest. No one has yet been able to come up with a solution that has the same rigour, elegance and functionality as the market-prices approach. But the inadequacy of mainstream economics at this point both accentuates the conceptual confusion (so that a political approach becomes synonymous with irrationality and arbitrariness) and encourages the spread not of science, but of the ideology of market economics (which is allowed simply to declare its 'opponent' to be illegitimate). We shall return later to the need for a rehabilitation of politics and its combination with a criterion of economic rationality.

THE SUBORDINATE STATE

Why has this provocative subheading been chosen to identify the more particular implications of the ideology we have just described?

The argument in this book has repeatedly based itself on a seemingly trivial yet highly embarrassing question. Does the notion of a general interest still have any meaning in a society ever more dominated by an economistic, market-centred mode of development, and subject to the constraints of 'globalization'? Part of an answer has already come from our discussion of the many problems arising at various community levels, from the local to the global. But this tells us nothing about the possible *content* of a general interest – unless, of course, the market logic, with its principles of solvent demand and profit accumulation, is made the sole, or the dominant, criterion in the organization of society. If the market is sanctified in this way, we have to look beyond the rhetoric of tackling poverty or assuring sustainable development, and beyond all the sincere or not so sincere declarations of benevolent intent. For the main task of the public authorities in neoliberal globalized modernity would then quite simply be to place themselves at the service of that market logic.

Such a conclusion has in fact been taken very seriously in recent years, as we can see from numerous cases of public intervention. Most of what follows will refer to the level of the national state. But this is only one of several levels to which these points apply, and perhaps the most instructive example of all is the birth, in this neoliberal context, of an official doctrine arguing the need for an international financial organization. Let us first, then, take a look at the World Bank, which may be considered the player with the greatest influence in guiding national and international development strategies. If we want to go beyond rhetoric and define the actual content of 'development' advocated by this institution, what better reference could there be than its own statutes and, in particular, the statement of aims contained within them? Now, Article 1 of the statutes of the core International Bank for Reconstruction and Development at the heart of the 'World Bank Group' – a text drafted and adopted at the July 1944 Bretton Woods Conference, and unaltered since – begins by alluding in general terms to 'development', then goes on to specify it as nothing other than the expansion of trade and international private investment. Here is this article in full (with emphasis added):

The purposes of the Bank are:

(i) To assist in the *reconstruction* and *development* of territories of members by facilitating the investment of capital for productive purposes, including the restoration of economies destroyed or disrupted by war, the reconversion of productive facilities to peacetime needs and the encouragement of the development of productive facilities and resources in less developed countries.

(ii) To *promote private foreign investment* by means of guarantees or participations in loans and other investments made by private investors; and when private capital is not available on reasonable terms, to supplement private investment by providing, on suitable conditions, finance for productive purposes out of its own capital, funds raised by it and its other resources.

(iii) To promote the long-range balanced growth of *international trade* and the maintenance of equilibrium in balances of payments by encouraging international investment for the development of the productive resources of members, thereby assisting in raising productivity, the standard of living and conditions of labour in their territories.

(iv) To arrange the loans made or guaranteed by it in relation to international loans through other channels so that the more useful and urgent projects, large and small alike, will be dealt with first.

(v) To conduct its operations with due regard to the effect of international investment on business conditions in the territories of members and, in the immediate postwar years, to assist in bringing about a smooth transition from a wartime to a peacetime economy.

The Bank shall be guided in all its decisions by the purposes set forth above.

It could hardly be clearer. The Bank is not mainly concerned with social progress (even if mention is made, rather curiously, of 'the standard of living' and 'the conditions of labour'); its priorities are not 'basic needs' or 'the struggle against poverty', as successive presidents have claimed in recent decades; its only concern is to support, through its investments, the productive, commercial and financial activity of the private sector. Let us repeat: the text has never been altered in more than half a century, and if it is scarcely ever quoted, this is undoubtedly because what it states is self-evident, despite the smokescreen of self-justificatory rhetoric.

Let us now turn to the level of the national state – although this does not mean that we are really leaving the World Bank, since again it is the Bank which offers us a particularly vivid demonstration of the relationship between state and market. In its official *World Development Report* for 1997,[2] the Bank considers 'the state in a changing world' – its thesis being that the state is subordinate to the forces and mechanisms of the market. This thesis, which I have called elsewhere the 'subordinate state' thesis,[3] may be summarized as follows.

The authors of the report first point out the error (and hardly anyone would deny that it is an error) of those who liked to think of development as the responsibility only of states. After recalling the practical failures that resulted from this approach both in the Eastern bloc and in some countries of the South, they immediately – and more surprisingly – go on to argue that those who called for the state to have only a minimal role in development were equally mistaken.

The next section of the report offers two arguments in support of a new public role in development: a classical outline of the 'failures' of market mechanisms, and a statement of why national public authorities are capable of intervening to remedy such defects. The arguments are so sensible that it seems impossible to assail them, but one cannot avoid pointing out that the position to which they lead is not far from the thesis of a minimal state. In fact, the institutional failings of the market and the state in relation to management of the economy sustain each other in a self-reinforcing process. The reasons for state intervention thus appear much clearer precisely where the state is the least capable of intervention, and much less compelling where the state does have such a capacity. In both cases, the situation tends to work against public intervention.

I shall not examine here the details of the argument as it is presented on each page of the report. It is, in my view, one of the most striking examples of that obsession with a single criterion for the management of economies and societies which has been repeatedly criticized above. In the World Bank version, the supporters of this ultra-liberal thesis no longer even feel the need to keep quiet about problems of 'environmental protection' or 'social justice' and redistribution (which explicitly feature in the table summarizing the argument of the report); no doubt this is why many observers thought they could detect a radical change of direction in World Bank doctrine. But although such problems are mentioned in theory, the force of the argument as a whole seems clearly opposed to any practical measures to address them. The reason for this is quite simply that, in keeping with tradition, the main concern of the report is to safeguard market mechanisms. If we are to judge by a document of this kind – or even by the long, controversial debate on the East Asian experience and the role of the state in development that was probably one of its sources[4] – then we have to recognize that relations between the state and the market are still a problem area, and that the difficulties will continue to increase if the general diagnosis suggested here on the impasses of modernity proves to be accurate. It is therefore all the more necessary that deeper thought should be given to the question.

THE QUEST FOR NEW CRITERIA

In Chapter 11, some markers will be suggested for a more realistic approach to the role of public authorities in relation to the market, development and the general interest. But, as with the four previous themes, we may already summarize the worst defects of the approach that has just been discussed.

1. However much common sense may be contained in the World Bank position, the first critical point concerns the simple need to be realistic in a world which, within the space of a few years, has witnessed the tragic events in Rwanda, Algeria, the former Yugoslavia and all too many other areas. It is high time that the debate on development, in the broad sense of a rational attempt to gain control of the evolution of human societies, should go beyond economistic approaches that argue only in terms of the relations between state and market, as if these were the only ways of regulating social life. It is time to refine the

simplistic view of the state as a neutral guardian of the general interest or a disruptively interventionist Leviathan, and the equally simplistic view (which virtually never comes true) of perfect market competition and resulting optimization. It is time to build in other ways of solving economic problems: especially through 'reciprocity' and gift-giving, but also through the life of the community, the new 'social movements',[5] and even the organization of personal and family life. Above all, it is time to go beyond the purely economic dimensions of social progress, in ways that take into account the quality of life, the authenticity and intensity of social relations, the forms of urban organization, respect for the identity of individuals and groups and their right to autonomy and security, and other social values that everyone recognizes as essential in theory but that are more or less disregarded in the present management of economies and societies. As we see, the point is always the same: to take into account the new complexity of economic and social life, and not to make it depend upon a single simplistic criterion, even if this is in the interests of certain groups or individuals.

2. The new criteria for public intervention in development should rest upon a dual basis, not just on an appreciation of the capacities of the state vis-à-vis the market (and especially not on a pre-established model that evaluates these two institutions as if they were homogeneous with each other). The first basis is *the specific aims of development*: a rigorous analysis of the 'effectiveness' of state intervention is possible only if it refers to the goals pursued by the state in question and by the societies for which it is responsible (effective in relation to what?), and therefore if it accepts the legitimacy of diversity in the choice of these goals. This point assumes, once again, the renunciation of a single standardized mode of development, even if it is a mode insistently recommended by the international organizations and the dominant players in the world economy. Above all, however, it assumes a mode of expressing social needs that is not in the thrall of solvent individual demand and the market maximization of profit.

The second basis is a rationalization of *public economic decisions* that is as rigorous as possible (though not necessarily absolved from market prices); it would have to conform as much as possible to the actual expression of social demand, but also cover the costs of responding to that demand (what I called above the 'solvency of society'). The difficulty here is not the principle of rationalization as such, which is today widely acknowledged, but the choice of methods to achieve it without reverting to the kind of 'marketization' of state action proposed by the

'New Public Management' school.[6] Much work remains to be done in this field to develop a range of specific indicators. For example, if the effectiveness of 'public safety' measures in the suburbs does not necessarily rise in proportion to the number of police officers keeping watch on the area, then various other indicators – crime figures, of course, but also perhaps the vigour of community life, the success of leisure centres, and so on – will need to be devised.

3. The argument that the only rigorous form of rationalization is based on market calculation and market prices is clearly unacceptable, because certain choices in the face of scarcity bring into play utilities and disutilities – or, if you like, benefits and costs – which cannot be made the object of market exchange, and therefore cannot be compared in terms of market prices. The inadequacy of the usual techniques of economic calculation does not mean that economic calculation is unnecessary, or that there is not a real problem of the allocation of scarce resources to satisfy alternative goals as well as possible. But to seek refuge in nothing other than market calculation is an easy option, whose rigour is only apparent, because it skates over the essence of what is at stake. The only acceptable course (even if it poses difficult problems of implementation) is to return to the 'basic' elements of an approach to any economic problem, whether or not it bears out the hypotheses of the market relationship, and to deduce from this an appropriate solution. It is ultimately this approach which justifies recourse to what used to be called 'planned development'. We shall return to it in the following chapters.

Paradoxically, it must also be said that the effects of the inadequacy of 'traditional' economics are aggravated by those who are supposed to use it to rationalize public choices. The situation may be described without caricature in the following way. The politicians responsible for setting the major guidelines are discouraged by the (real or apparent) technical complexity of the choices to be made. They therefore rely entirely on 'expert' advisers who think as technicians (engineers or economists) and mostly use what they have already mastered rather than risk developing other techniques – which means that, in economic matters, they limit themselves to the most orthodox approaches that have been most extensively tested by the market. This involves a kind of two-stage reductionism – from politics to economics, and from economics to market economics – which is not unrelated to the growing scepticism in 'development circles' about the rigour of public economics, and to the consequent strengthening of the ideological influence and practical methods of market economics.

CONCLUSION

As in the case of the previous problems we have discussed, only perhaps even more so, the role of the public authorities is an extremely complicated issue that has very broad implications for the analysis of modernity and the political debate on its evolution. For the moment, I would just like to conclude these first general considerations by underlining a particularly striking paradox: the contrast between the current situation of many public bodies around the world, and the crucial importance of this whole problem in the ideological context of neoliberalism.

The facts are rather discouraging. At an international level, despite the power of such major organizations as the Bretton Woods financial and commercial institutions, the World Trade Organization, and at a more local level the European Union, *the world economy remains fundamentally unregulated*. Or, to be more precise, despite the piling up of bureaucratic regulations and requirements, the existing institutions do not yet seem capable of addressing the real problems of public interest that result from the operation of the world economy.

These institutions do, of course, manage what exists at present; they often play the role of 'policemen', support some favourable trends, and correct some abuses. But their actions remain skewed by the dominant interests in the world economy, and by a concern to maintain the global system that works to their advantage. In the best of cases, measures that are said to benefit the majority of the world's population tackle the consequences rather than the structural causes of the problems in the system. It might be objected that national states have rarely done anything else, and that no one, apart from a few hypocrites or a few unrepentant idealists, believes any longer that the state is the true guardian of the general interest. This is undoubtedly true. But the real problem, which has kept cropping up in our analysis, is the new and fantastically enlarged dimension of the human issues in a globalized economy, and therefore the urgent need for a vision capable of rising above the antagonisms of short-term particular interests. It is the lack of such a vision of the future beyond the limits of the dominant system that casts doubt upon the extent to which the world economy is presently regulated.

With regard to national states, it would obviously be rather inappropriate to put forward a uniform diagnosis, still less to complain of their numerous inadequacies (most of which are hardly new). But it has to be admitted that their task has also become formidably complex. This probably explains two further phenomena: the fact that even the more 'presentable' national states lack an overall picture of the long-term challenges which no one seems to be really on top of; and the disturbing spread of violent forms of 'predatory' state, or of states that are incapable of defending such basic public interests as law and order, the protection of minorities and the suppression of large-scale crime.

These ever more glaring defects of public authorities, both national and international, contrast with the dominant discourse of neoliberal ideology and its refusal to expand the role of collective institutions. For if the above analysis were to be summarized in one basic characteristic, it would be the increased complexity of what is at stake in the functioning of the economy in society, and the growing number of collective problems linked with that complexity. The paradox stems from the fact that these collective problems cannot be solved through market mechanisms alone.

In this light, the need for new public responsibilities is not just one theme of debate among others; it is the very heart of the analysis and the political proposals considered throughout this book. For the point is not to repeat the traditional observations about the shortcomings of government, but to understand the nature and the dimension of the new issues at stake, and to grasp that a new distribution of decision-making powers is an inescapable necessity within modern economies.

This is true even if – indeed, especially if – one accepts the basic virtues of a market economy. As neoliberal modernity becomes global, the task still remaining is truly enormous.

PART THREE

INTRODUCTION TO THE POLITICAL DEBATE

THE RESULTS SO FAR:
A CONTRADICTORY AND ALIENATING
MODERNITY WITHOUT A FUTURE

> On the face of it, far from being a 'natural' system, as some apologists
> have tried to argue, historical capitalism is a patently absurd one. One
> accumulates capital in order to accumulate more capital. Capitalists are
> like white mice on a treadmill, running ever faster in order to run still
> faster.
>
> Immanuel Wallerstein, *Historical Capitalism*, p. 40.

The following four conclusions may be provisionally drawn from the
preceding chapters.

1. Our analysis of the nature and consequences of modernity has sought
to draw out the general underlying logics of progress, market, profit,
accumulation and power. Within this perspective, the first point to make
concerns the one-dimensional character of the social system dominated
by economics, such that, faced with the growing complexity of human
societies, it persistently subordinates their organizational requirements
to the single criterion of individually appropriable profit.

The presence of these logics, however, does not allow us to assume
that the system is perfectly regulated – on the contrary, a number of
contradictions and obstacles testify to a major lack of regulation and,
on any scenario, threaten the indefinite continuation of these overall
logics. These obstacles, though diverse in nature, are all the more
worrying because of the danger that they will mutually reinforce one
another. Those analysed here directly affect economic, social and ecological equilibria.

Economic equilibria are affected because the very idea of indefinitely growing output in a world of finite resources is contradictory, because global competition impels each country to reduce its internal costs and demand so that it can export more – which eventually, as in the case of agriculture, reinforces monopoly situations in the name of free competition – and because the financial economy becomes divorced from the real economy in respect of decision-making criteria but not of the consequences they entail. All these factors lead to symptoms of inefficiency that negate the system's claims to be economically rigorous.

Social equilibria are affected because the growth dynamic, as well as the dynamics of need creation, competition and profit accumulation that determine its shape, entail a greater concentration of wealth, a sharpening of inequality, and a proliferation of the processes of exclusion and marginalization. These phenomena of concentration, inequality and exclusion sustain one another, and eventually erode the minimal degree of cohesion, the capacity for self-determination, necessary for society to assume its own destiny, and even to remain viable in the long run.

Ecological equilibria are affected because the indefinite growth of production, apparently inevitable if the system is to survive, requires an industrialization of productive activity which can be achieved only at the cost of accelerated consumption of the stock of non-renewable resources. The historically unprecedented level of such consumption in recent decades cannot, however, be prolonged in time or generalized in space.

2. These general contradictions are clearly not the only ones observable in the system that has grown out of modernity. Indeed, our brief studies of growth, inequality, work, international exchange and the role of public authorities have revealed a series of paradoxes that illustrate these general contradictions and intensify this contradictory character. Let us recall some of the most important paradoxes:

- The obsession with precise economic calculation, in the name of a rigour that is rarely respected in practice (as Paul Krugman has shown[7]); the claim to rationality, contrasting with a deliberate limitation of economic calculation to the elements of social evolution that lend themselves to market calculation; hence an astonishing lack of overall vision and mastery of the system, with regard to its total effect on the biosphere, social relations, the viability of societies, and peace among men;

• the radical and surprisingly inhuman character of the split between economic and social development; the imbalance of power between local and global decision-making bodies, in a development system which claims to be serving social progress, and therefore real men and women, but which in the end treats them as mere cogs in the productive machine, and is tempted to pass them by altogether whenever possible;

• the maintenance of employed status as a virtual *sine qua non* for access to consumption, while the evolution of the system itself is marked by increasing capital intensity in most sectors and hence a decline in opportunities for paid work, together with graver consequences of unemployment for the living conditions of a growing section of the population;

• the increase in community needs engendered by the system itself, which is not surprising, since the system takes into account only the individual market variables of the economic problem but ignores its collective dimensions, especially the unintended effects of supposedly rational individual behaviour; fierce opposition on ideological grounds to the establishment – sometimes even the maintenance – of community or public institutions that are alone capable of adequately responding to these new collective needs.

When all is said and done, no one denies that the system has proved exceptionally capable in mobilizing resources, producing goods and services, and therefore responding to needs and transforming living standards. But it is understood today that the system has both positive and negative aspects, that it generates both development and underdevelopment. And the dizziness produced by these contradictions suggests a question that is troubling, to say the least. For is not the system in the grip of madness, as it speeds up the destruction of its own resources and sacrifices the future, constantly creating artificial new needs, yet less and less satisfying basic needs for a growing proportion of the world's population? No one seems to know where it is leading us, and still less whether it can be brought under control.

This is certainly not the first time that an economic, social and political system has lacked internal coherence and proven incapable of mastering its own future. Before the middle of the twentieth century, Arnold Toynbee was already interpreting History as a succession of civilizations that have each known a rise, an apogee and a decline.[8] So, there's nothing new under the sun? That is not so certain. For the present system is no doubt the first in history which not only claims sway over the whole planet, but engages in a periodic felling of planetary resources with major and irreversible consequences. In this sense, although globalization is but the acceleration of an already existing logic, it is still an entirely new phenomenon in the history of humanity. If the system is mad, it is all the more necessary to understand the extent of that madness.

This is why it is essential to deepen our critical analysis of the system in all its dimensions, well beyond the preliminary remarks that have been offered here. But the most urgent task, perhaps, is to develop a genuine political debate about the principles, the functioning and the consequences of this global system, within a 'meta-economic' perspective that gets to the heart of the economic preoccupations governing the system, yet also takes the analysis further to examine the consequences of 'economism' for the prevailing values, culture, social structures and political organization. The following pages will consider what is required for such a political debate to take place; they will also try to start some discussion of the dominant system of values and the need for new directions, as well as proposing some initial elements of an alternative politics.

3. We should not, however, be under any illusion. The very idea of sparking off a political debate on all these questions will run up against formidable difficulties. Let us begin by simply recalling the difficulty bound up with the available apparatus of concepts and policies – for it will be necessary to shake off the 'traditional' platitudes, skewed visions and false promises deployed by most 'experts' in the field of development. The traditional analysis is formulated mainly in macroeconomic terms, and the macroeconomic schemas accepted by the most powerful international organizations (the World Bank or the OECD, for example), which are virtually alone in having the means to collect and synthesize global information, remain desperately poor and rigid in their conservatism. The efforts of the United Nations Development Programme have, it is true, brought remarkable progress in this area, but those mainly responsible for them recognize that a long road lies ahead.

But there are even more serious difficulties. Although the analysis proposed in previous chapters is still only rudimentary, its first results show clearly enough the profoundly alienating character of modernity when it appears with the features that have just been outlined. It is alienating in the gravest sense of robbing individuals and social groups of control over their own destiny: first, because it deflects the expression of needs towards individual solvent demand, and especially towards the solvent demand of the most powerful players (unless the needs are interpreted by unaccountable technocrats who are themselves subject to the forces dominating the market); second, because the elements that constitute the life of society are systematically destroyed if they do not conform to the rules of the market relation; and third, because individuals are ultimately conditioned by a system of values, needs and responses to needs which is entirely manufactured by a few dominant interests. This alienation is, as we have seen, greatly reinforced by the process of accelerated globalization, and by the distance this sets up between individuals and social groups, on the one hand, and the centres of world economic decision-making, on the other.

This value system of modernity does not have much in common with the deepest exigencies of life in society, nor with the most legitimate needs of the human condition. Yet it does not shrink from any means of imposing its domination: the lies of advertising and the thousand forms of packaged imitation; arguments based on authority and supposed competence; exclusion, poverty and denial of identity; sometimes even war, death squads and ethnic cleansing. The calm supremacy of the ruling ideology – surprisingly little contested in the leading circles of any political tendencies – is doubtless the best testimony to the success of this enterprise. It is not certain that this success will last in the long term, however, if we are to judge by the first signs of a deep split between men, women, public opinion and social associations, on the one hand, and the dominant players in corporations, the world of politics, international technocracies and most of the media, on the other.

4. The fourth and most disturbing conclusion, then, concerns the high degree of hypocrisy in the thinking of governments, multilateral organizations and transnational corporations, but also of public and private development agencies, which would have us believe that the whole of humanity is marching inevitably towards 'development' and 'modernity', defined in accordance with the Western experience. In reality, the evidence strongly shows that the globalization of modernity does not have a long-term future, mainly for economic, social and ecological reasons, and that a different way of conceiving the future is therefore necessary.

This preliminary conclusion confirms our initial sense that an impasse has been reached in which there is no overall control. Worse: neoliberal modernity seems doomed practically because it leads to a number of impasses, and doomed politically because it is morally unacceptable.

If we are to go beyond this negative critique, and seek out alternative paths, we will obviously have to begin a profound change in our way of thinking. Such a change has to be first of all political, since it primarily concerns not means, constraints and ways of managing constraints but, rather, the characteristics of the society we want to foster, and therefore the goals and values around which it is organized and which it tends to defend and implement.

All I claim to be proposing here are the first tentative steps in this quest. The following chapters will underline the urgency of the political debate and what are its main requirements; then outline a critical (first negative, later positive) consideration of the value system underlying present modernity and of changes in that system which might ground alternative paths to modernity. The final chapter will look more closely at some specific questions for the political debate as such and sketch some initial elements of an alternative policy.

CHAPTER 11

REASONS, NATURE AND REQUIREMENTS OF THE POLITICAL DEBATE

What should advocates of a practical political philosophy be doing? They must analyse, criticize, refine and revise the values and commitments of their contemporaries, then they must honestly describe the difficulties that those values and commitments encounter in today's world: the nature of the opposition, the sites of political struggle, the institutional obstacles, and the broad lines of the necessary reforms.

Michael Walzer, *Pluralisme et démocratie*, p. 149.

Today, instead of dodging the issues, we must prove that we are still able to choose.

Dominique Méda, *Qu'est-ce que la richesse?*, p. 11.

The really urgent question, then, is the restoration of politics. More precisely, the task is to revive the interest of citizens in public debate, to restore the credibility of the public authorities, to reform the rules of the political game so that they no longer encourage immobility or clientelism, to renew the dialogue between electors and elected, to rehabilitate debate over ideas and our vision of the world ahead. In short, we must change politics.

Jacques Généreux, *Une raison d'espérer*, p. 164.

A DEBATE FOR WHAT PURPOSE?

The hold of modernity and globalization appears to be so extensive, even totalitarian, that it has managed to discourage political debate. The refusal to engage in discussion is not just limited to the dominant players in the global system (who have an obvious interest in disarming any opposition to a process that works to their advantage); it sadly also reflects a kind of fatalistic resignation that is widespread among political leaders and organizational managers, as well as in public opinion and the media that influence it.

For those who take this attitude, neoliberal globalization is an indisputable and irreversible fact; no doubt one can either welcome or
fear its consequences, but there is no other option than to adapt to it
– actively in the case of the strongest, who can profit from the opportunities it opens up; or passively in the case of the weakest, as a way of
trying to limit the damage. What cannot be envisaged is any action
affecting the globalization process itself, or its major consequences.

The political reflections offered here are opposed to such a pessimistic
view: they start from the very different idea that the logic of globalization is of human origin, and by no means irreversible. But they also
reject any illusion about the obstacles in the way of change, or about
the possibility of overturning the world order through a few inspired
or not-so-inspired verbal declarations. Nor do they accept that partial
technical solutions are feasible, or that a simple concern to improve the
way the system is run can suffice to get it back on course, or to
extricate it from the impasses in which it is stuck.

We have to be clear about the unusual scale of the change in
approach that is needed. For the analysis in this book claims both to
offer a radical general critique of the reality we can observe around us,
and to emerge with a positive perspective of hope rather than an
admission of impotence. Its diagnosis concerning the present forms of
modernity and the dominant model of development is very negative,
because they seem to be without a future and morally unacceptable.
But it asserts more strongly than ever both the necessity and the possibility of social progress, and it is unequivocally committed to the
quest for a different mode of development.

What is proposed here, then, is not a kind of rhetorical last-ditch
stand; it is based on the profound conviction that other paths can and
must be explored. The analysis has also made it clear that the impasses
of modernity derive largely from the fact that we have allowed ourselves to be boxed in by words, by slogans whose content we have not
tried to clarify, and by methods of conceptualization, accounting and
analysis which distort social reality. We have let ourselves be trapped –
or, to be more precise, 'alienated' – by constraints which, though
certainly real and present, have been wrongly taken as divine decrees,
or at least as imperatives inherent in the nature of the world and the
'inescapable' laws of economics. For in fact, these constraints are the
results (intentional or unintentional) of human decisions that it is
possible for us to question, at least partially and on certain conditions.

Let us specify what those conditions are. I believe that if these constraints and imperatives are assessed in a new light, neoliberal global-

ization and the model of modernity it disseminates cannot appear either
as the radiant hope for the future (the century now ending has been
filled with such promises, mostly destined to collapse) or as the inevitable prelude to a new totalitarian nightmare. Above all, I believe
that pluralism is a possibility. In other words, I would like to believe
that globalization and modernity can still be transformed into models
open to a plurality of content, provided that we consider them as such
and initiate the kind of political debate this requires (even if the debate
has to be limited, and must proceed in stages over a very long period).

No one, I think, knows the exact solution to the problems raised
here. I will therefore keep to a few general points by way of long-term
orientation and not suggest any formulas that can be immediately
applied. Further reflection along these lines will have to involve a much
greater effort to sharpen our intellectual-analytical tools and to think
about reality in a different way.[1] It will also have to make more systematic use of the theoretical work and collective experiments accumulated
in the past – although the practice of the social sciences strikes me,
alas, as peculiarly resistant to these requirements, and each specialist
seems to think he or she can reconstruct the world as on the first day
of Genesis.[2] One last point is that such a start at general reflection
makes sense only if it is then taken up and continued at the level of
each of the actual communities concerned.

A PLAN FOR SOCIETY AND THE
ETHICAL QUEST FOR MEANING

Since our analysis has tried to identify the general logic of the dominant
model of development, and to describe the social vision resulting from
it, the present political debate must focus on an alternative plan for
society and the quest for an alternative vision and logic; it cannot, in
other words, be a discussion among technicians about the implementation of a set of objectives laid down by a higher authority.

The term 'plan for society' is hardly precise, and is perhaps being
wrongly used, but it should at least enable us to make quite a sharp
distinction. A debate about society is not a debate about the means
whereby a community can achieve a goal set from outside it; the point
here is to debate the actual collective goals to be chosen and the general
shape of society corresponding to them. The approach is, in essence,
political: that is, it concerns people's aims, and takes into account the
various interests present within society; it analyses the options available,

works out the ways in which conflicts between them can be settled, and formulates what they imply for the community; and it requires the gradual construction of an overall vision of the common good or the general interest, freely decided by the community in question.[3]

In the end, then, we are talking about a quest for meaning – which is what is required by the analysis of an alienating and contradictory system without a future. But this quest is at the opposite pole from the one touted in the name of resignation by the alienating modernity and globalization that have just been described. It is a quest that is politically opposed to the dominant way of thinking, of course, because it rejects the claims of neoliberal globalization to sow uniformity and domination, as well as the imitative character of the modernity and the development advocated by the champions of such globalization. In fact, it is also opposed to them as a matter of theoretical principle, because the liberal-individualist philosophy of the dominant model identifies the general interest with the sum of particular interests mediated by the market and can therefore see no basis for a collective debate about aims. This suppression of political debate has finally led to confusion in development theories, where a multiplication of qualifying epithets has become necessary ('human development', 'social development', 'sustainable development', etc.) and, more generally, various moral concerns have re-emerged after a period when they were driven out by the very nature of liberal 'optimization' ('the market is not immoral, but non-moral').

A FRESH LOOK AT THE FOUNDATIONS OF POLITICS AND ECONOMICS

At this point, we need to step back and make a certain effort at abstraction before turning to particular aspects of political reorientation. For a debate on collective goals implies nothing less than a review of the very foundations of the social order. The analysis so far suggests that three requirements need to be met in this regard.

1. The whole of the economic and social system must be repositioned in relation to human aspirations, for it is made for people as individuals and members of a group, not vice versa. But this system constructed for men and women must also be put back in its proper place vis-à-vis all living things, vis-à-vis the whole of the biosphere and the ecosystem. We do not have to turn nature into something sacred for us to see that human beings cannot permit themselves everything.

2. Within this system, the economy must be repositioned in a subordinate relation to society. We have already mentioned Louis Dumont's fears of a danger of political and social totalitarianism, and it is enough to consider the history of the twentieth century to realize that they are not without foundation. But the supremacy of the economy and market criteria in social life has reached a point where a different kind of totalitarianism, as undesirable as the first, is to be feared. This is why the economy must be placed at the service of society, and therefore of the conception of politics that it develops and defends.

3. Market economics must be repositioned in relation to economics in general. It is true that the political order is also subject to a requirement of economic viability, but the criteria of such a rationalization of the 'collective' economy are not quite the same as those of the market economy. In other words, it is necessary to redefine the foundations of 'general' economic analysis, in such a way that it is no longer reduced to the criteria of profit, solvent demand, private appropriation and rivalry.

Should these three requirements for the debate be regarded merely as convenient generalizations, too abstract to be of any practical consequence? I do not think so. Applied to the everyday running of economies and societies, they are the exact opposite of the recommendations offered by the dominant wisdom – especially by the international organizations, which think that the basic problems of the world system can be solved through 'good governance', or greater rigour in applying economic orthodoxy, or contorted verbal incantations about 'user-friendly markets', a 'social market economy' or 'civic enterprise'. By contrast, our three requirements challenge the foundations of this system in overall terms, but they also attack the particular mode of decision-making within the system, and especially the principle of the indefinite accumulation of profit as the sole criterion for choices in economic and social organization.

Theory lovers will probably argue that the intention of this critique is to bring about a veritable 'paradigm shift'. Much more practically, however, it implies that the impasse diagnosed above cannot be overcome through 'managerial' improvements; that a solution can be found only if the problem is conceived and formulated in a fundamentally new way, both at a general level and in terms of specific decisions.

Evidently such a debate relates back to a discussion of 'values'. For the economic and social system cannot give a meaning to our civilization (or make our development 'sustainable', to use the fashionable jargon) unless it is grounded upon a new morality of social needs, opposed to the dynamic of unlimited individual and material needs that is the basis of dominant modernity. This discussion of values, already touched upon several times in previous chapters, will be taken up more synthetically in the next chapter.

LACK OF REALISM?

> It is often said that force is powerless to overcome thought; but for this to be true, there must be thought.
> Simone Weil, *Oppression and Liberty*, p. 119.

More serious than the charge of abstraction is the argument that a debate defined in the terms we have just used is lacking in realism. Indeed, the very idea of such an ambitious debate will probably be dismissed not only by all the 'managers' with more pressing things on their mind, but also by many 'sensible' people who think it better to take effective action than to go on discussing for evermore. Yet my answer is the same as to the previous objection. I think we need more than ever to stand back and analyse; I do not trust the urge to be immediately effective in a field of such complexity. The reason for this lies in the very nature of the present impasse, and in the crucial importance of a new way of seeing things. Once again, the question is not whether the system will change or not; a change will certainly come about, even if not tomorrow, because the existing system does not have a long-term future. Rather, the question is: what will be the conditions under which that change occurs? To what extent will it be controlled? And, above all, in whose interests will it take place? This is being realistic.

Integration for a minority plus exclusion for a majority is a twin tendency that has many chances of continuing, even of growing more intense. The task ahead, therefore, is to challenge the existing forms of hegemony and to turn around the existing relationship of forces, but also to formulate the problem in different terms. Without that, no solution can be envisaged.

Such a turnaround can obviously be imagined only in the long term – not only because of its complexity and difficulty, but quite simply because it involves the transformation of a historical tendency and a culture which rest upon several centuries of tradition, and because the long-term viability of human societies and of the earth's biosphere is at stake. To adopt a long-term perspective, however, does not mean postponing action until later. On the contrary, there is an urgent need right now to begin changing the directions analysed above.

The political and social base – that is, the structure of social groups, interests and political forces, with their capacities for analysis and action – might serve to explain or support the emergence of one alternative or another, and of course it is necessary to keep underlining the importance of gradually raising the consciousness of the whole of society and of all social groups in relation to the changes that are needed. But such a general movement will not be enough. It is also necessary to keep underlining the special interest of the most underprivileged social groups – whether they are particular countries, regions, age groups, occupational categories, social classes, ethnic and religious minorities, or whatever – because these groups are the first victims of the current intensification of inequality and exclusion. But once again, the raising of consciousness will not be sufficient to make up for the insufficiency of power. Each society, therefore, must think in terms of developing more precise, more specific strategies, by identifying the groups which are the clearest 'bearers' of change and the most capable of bringing it about. It must locate those who are already practising economic and social activities outside the profit criterion – in national or international public services, of course, but also in cultural pursuits, neighbourhood or village associations, 'local exchange trading systems' (LETS), or groups that address particularly urgent problems in the life of society. Naturally, these remarks do not exclude those with formal responsibility for macroeconomic or macrosocial activities or for the running of large companies. But, in the face of globalization, they do suggest that it is important to attach far greater value to the local level of social life.

This brings us to a final point about the organization of the political debate: the need to go beyond fundamental reflection and academic discussion (essential stages though they are) and to establish a close link with *social practices*. The concepts and arguments of the dominant theory do have to be reworked, together with its logic, its criteria and its language, since that whole apparatus makes us incapable of conceptualizing, connecting and solving certain essential problems of society. This conceptual and theoretical labour risks being in vain, however, if it does not base itself much more than in the past upon the real aspirations and practices of individuals and groups, especially upon the many initiatives through which societies are today seeking to escape the verbal traps and mystifications of the dominant thinking. All too often a gulf still separates theoretical reflection and practical experience; there are very few institutional or other sites (whether parliaments, parties, trade unions, associations, universities or media) which allow the two to come into contact with each other at a sufficiently profound level.

CHAPTER 12

THE QUESTION OF VALUES

What is a rebel? A man who says no; but whose refusal does not imply a renunciation. He is also a man who says yes as soon as he begins to think for himself.

Albert Camus, *The Rebel*, p. 19.

A change of economic and social system assumes a change of the value system upon which it is based. This problem has already been mentioned several times, and in this chapter I intend to tackle it by first identifying the dominant values of the existing system, then considering some of the alternative values that might take their place. But a brief warning about method is in order here. Can one really claim to identify these dominant values – and, if so, how?

The existing system, with its fairly wide consensus (spontaneous or imposed), directly governs the current perceptions and practical behaviour of individuals and communities. It thus concerns such fundamental questions and attitudes as those relating to life and death, work and leisure, time and nature, individual, family and group, freedom and hierarchy, affluence and poverty, material wealth and money. But it is not necessarily the object of sophisticated intellectual articulation, or even of any coherent and explicit representation, and it is therefore difficult to locate its values in a way that leaves no room for dispute. Constantly evolving in history, the system can never be captured in a snapshot;[1] and the society to which it refers is not a homogeneous bloc but an ensemble of specific social groups, each of which incorporates or repudiates in varying degrees the dominant values.[2] Most important of all, perhaps, the confusion of ends and means in the economic and social system of modernity is not conducive to clarity about its reference values, and indeed actually encourages its dominant players to 'instrumentalize' the final values (democracy, welfare, self-affirmation, and so on) so that they serve their own particular interests.[3]

I do not intend to discuss these difficulties and the possible solutions in detail here. One promising approach does deserve to be mentioned, however, which might be compared to the economists' technique of 'revealed preferences analysis'. Essentially, this sets out to analyse the observable results of individual and collective behaviour, rather than the discourse and statements claiming to announce or justify it. Certain governments and international organizations never stop talking of 'democracy', although the procedures they actually use are systematically authoritarian; certain groups preach nothing but virtue and practise nothing but corruption, or claim to be disinterested when their only aim is enrichment, or are full of praise for investment when all they do is consume. Obvious truths? Maybe. But this approach does have the advantage of basing the study of dominant values upon facts of observation, both quantifiable aggregates (structure of output and expenditure, consumption model, income distribution) and the role of institutions and game rules particularly indicative of the dominant values (private property, labour legislation, tax system, and so on). Analysis of these aspects is not without consequence, and it can begin the process of demystification necessary for any change in the value system.

AN INVENTORY OF THE
DOMINANT VALUES IN PLAY

Let us now attempt the description to which we referred above. This will not be a detailed or exhaustive inventory, of course, but will briefly locate the broad categories of values directly linked with the history of modernity, and especially with its economic dimensions.[4]

The main emphasis will be on five constitutive values of modernity: the general belief in progress; the materialist, and later financial, expression of this conception of progress; the central place of productive labour, and of efficiency and (at least instrumental) 'rationality'; individual self-assertion in the face of the group and community, including its political organization; and a blanket affirmation of ethnocentric certainties.

Belief in social progress is the core value of modernity: men and societies are perfectible, perhaps even more so tomorrow than today; history does not have the character of a repetitive cycle, of an 'eternal return'.

The ideology of 'development' – which has been driving the world since the end of the Second World War, and which no state would dare renounce today – is thus a continuation of the Enlightenment and the West European Industrial Revolution.[5] But when one tries to be more precise about this category of values, the concept of development raises at least three crucial questions to which modern societies mostly avoid giving explicit answers.

- The first question concerns the content and the measure of development. Does it mainly refer to the welfare of whole populations (measured by income level or more detailed indicators), to the growth of commodity production and profitable 'business', to the power of states, political leaders and a privileged elite, or to all of these at once?
- Second, it is necessary to consider the distribution of the fruits of development. Can this be relatively equitable and egalitarian, or is the development of some necessarily built upon the underdevelopment and poverty of others?
- Third and last, there is the problem of specifying a time horizon. For whereas social progress makes sense, and development can be evaluated and programmed, only over a long period of time, the current conception of economics, geared to profitability, clearly rests upon the very short term and a 'preference for the present', without explicitly taking into account the eventual consequences.

Materialism and *marketization* largely determine the kind of answers that are given to these three questions, reducing social progress to material prosperity and converting the challenge of development into a mainly economic problem of the allocation of scarce resources and the private appropriation of products. The characteristic preoccupations are thus with productivity, growth and profitability, while the consequences for power and income inequalities and for longer-term interests are left out of account.

Furthermore, in a modernity dominated by market forces, prosperity hinges on the total amount of commodities and market services that *individuals* can appropriate with their existing purchasing power (that is, with their wealth or income).

Homogenization in terms of money makes it possible to measure this total quantity through the system of prices, so that an increased value of production (and of income corresponding to it) becomes the main indicator of this type of development. We thus reach the core of the values that we are trying to identify; it is essentially the *relationship to money* which governs the value system in an economy dominated by market relations. In capitalism, this relationship to money is itself dominated by the indefinite accumulation of profit, which – as we have seen – is the main, if not the only, criterion of the organization of 'market society' in all its components (most especially at the level of the firm, where profit maximization in the short-term management of finances seems to outweigh all other considerations). The *sanctification of private property* may be understood as a necessary institutional condition of the market relation and the accumulation of profit, but it adds to these a social guarantee of *security* for certain individuals. In the end, then, the precedence of profit over any other criterion of decision-making is the crux of the relationship between value system and economic and social organization.

If progress is measured only by the value of production for the market (goods and services), and if individual income is the principal means of gaining access to those commodities, then we can see why *productive labour* also features among the central values that serve as the reference for social organization. It is a value with an ancient heritage, going back to Genesis and to the Christian conception of the world as a set of tasks for man to fulfil, but it has been considerably strengthened by the capitalist mobilization for growth, and by the process of marketization, which means that, for most people, paid labour is a precondition for enjoying its fruits. This emphasis on labour gives a single meaning to the whole of each individual's life, so that periods of education and training are viewed not in terms of personal or collective fulfilment but only in relation to future labour productivity.

However, the technological advances that permitted the emergence of this modernity have had the effect that, outside the service sector, labour is no longer (with land) the dominant element in the combination of productive factors; physical and financial capital, perhaps even more knowledge and information, have occupied that position. The concern for productive efficiency, virtually identified with financial profitability, now applies to the whole of this combination of factors. Hence the ever-present concern with rationality, and the claim that the system represents a higher, or even the ultimate, form of rationalization of human behaviour.

Yet this form remains specific, in the sense that it refuses to entertain any questions about its own purpose. The rationality of the system of capitalist modernity thus presents itself as an *instrumental* rationality, geared primarily to profit and, perhaps more broadly, to power.

The values we have just identified confirm the essentially *individualist* philosophy of the system based upon them. Exalted by the Enlightenment, the individual remains the reference unit in this organization of society, in spite of the alienation (that is, the growing loss of control by individuals over their own fate) which it generates. The 'private' economic interests of the individual (as consumer, producer, trader, capitalist, speculator, rentier) are supposed to be the sole aim of the market relation. But it actually claims to supplant *every* other social bond and *every* other means of pursuing the general interest within a now 'atomized' society. Despite all proof to the contrary, the interests of the individual are held to be 'private', on the grounds that they are ostensibly free of any link with a social group or any collective representation. This idyllic view of the market ignores the conditioning effects of imitation, and more generally of alienation, which are 'inseparable from the rise of mass production', as George Steiner eloquently shows in relation to the 'crisis of culture'.[6] It also ignores the various cumulative mechanisms which transform the (in principle legitimate) play of the market into an ever more constrictive and invasive totalitarian logic. In particular, it ignores the mechanisms of cumulative inequality, so that paradoxically it is leading to a kind of 'inegalitarian consensus' (that is, an at least passive acceptance of the situation of inequality[7]). In fact, it regards such an outcome as inevitable, even claiming that it is in accordance with its own basic values.

The individual is supposed to be autonomous and, as such, to enjoy entrepreneurial freedom as well as consumer sovereignty. But – for reasons linked both with an avowedly humanist philosophy and with the practical demands of human societies (especially in terms of public order) – the individual is also a citizen endowed with responsibility in the democratic organization of a law-governed state. Such a state has also been one of the crucial demands of modernity, which has thus acquired a public dimension. Yet the recent evolution of neoliberal modernity towards an ever more assertive supremacy of economic concerns has consecrated and generalized the predominance of private values over public values. And it is not certain that democracy, however loud the fanfares that always announce it, will really get anything out of this evolution, and the accompanying subordination of the state and other public bodies to private interests.

Whether these interests are weak or powerful, they call on the state only when they demand rights and protection (never obligations) for themselves. The very idea of collective responsibility – of a concern for

the negative collective effects of (even innocent) individual behaviour –
is fundamentally alien to neoliberal modernity.

The last main feature of the value system of modernity is eloquently
condemned in Jean-Claude Guillebaud's *La Trahison des Lumières*.[8] He
shows that modernity was originally a product of the West's capacity
for self-criticism, that it corresponded to a concern for greater openness, and that it was conceived as a set of *questions*. These qualities were
soon distorted as the desire for expansion led to colonization and
imperialism, and Western arrogance came to saturate history over the
centuries. Beneath the faded globalist or humanist finery, it is still the
same certainty and the same arrogance which prevail in our own times.
The self-criticism, openness and questioning have not, it is true, disappeared from the scene. But for practical, productivist reasons, they
have made way for the certainties of managerial authoritarianism, for
the brutal assertion of privilege by the rich and powerful, and ultimately
for the ethnocentric *Westernization* of the world – even when market
values appear to have been 'reappropriated' outside the West.[9] Market
and neoliberal globalization can then be presented as the only, compulsory path to progress.

WHAT A DIFFERENT ETHIC MIGHT INVOLVE

This value system, as we have summarized it here, seems to be solidly
built. Is it not unrealistic, or quite simply a non-starter, to imagine that
it could be transformed?

I am not so naive as to think that a value system and a culture can
be transformed by decree, especially when they are becoming global in
reach. I am simply trying to further what appears to me an urgent
process of ethical reflection. This cannot go beyond some very general
principles, precisely because it repudiates the arrogant but convenient
totalitarianism of a globalization that claims to be inevitable. I shall
therefore limit myself to three kinds of points regarding the construction
of a different ethic; they will be negative, positive and interrogative, in
that order. But first, we cannot avoid grappling with a question that
often remains only implicit in such debates. Are there universal, or at
least 'universalizable', values?

The development of universal values – or, in other words, of a
'single scale of values' (Walzer), at least in some areas – may strike us as
such a formidable task (in terms of both conceptual definition and
cultural-political acceptance) that it, too, tends to discourage the initia-

tion of political debate. It assumes a certain transcendence, an affirmation of indisputable principles or norms, a capacity for stepping back, and even a certain pluralism in areas that are not directly affected by 'indisputable' values. This principle of pluralism conflicts, of course, with the authoritarianism of the West and its 'culture of contentment', but the real difficulty is to define the boundaries of such a principle.

In terms of economic and social organization, the emergence of universal values implies the rejection of any single criterion specific to a particular civilization; this is evidently the case with the criterion of appropriable profit, but the principle also applies to the rejection of economic growth at any price, because of the privilege this entails for a minority and the social and ecological costs for a majority. Universal values thus require at least some definition of social justice – but the criteria of social justice are still far from unanimous[10] – and of the requirements of solidarity with regard to the basic needs of all. All this seems immensely difficult to spell out in precise detail, and even more to integrate into a universal consensus. It is perhaps too soon – yet it is very late in the day.

Let us not give in once more to the illusion peculiar to Western culture and import so-called 'rationality' where it has nothing to say. The question of 'values' does not come within the province of rationality; nor in the end does moral behaviour. It is not a criterion of rationality – and certainly not a criterion of economic rationality – that will clarify to what extent income inequalities, for example, are morally tolerable in a given society. In this perspective, many observers (among whom I would be tempted to include myself) do not think that many tangible results can be expected from a discussion about universal values, apart from the evident but necessary positive principle of value pluralism, and apart from the negative principle of the 'prohibition of the inhuman' (Walzer) or, as I propose to call it, the rejection of the unacceptable.

I am well aware that this latter principle only really shifts the problem elsewhere, since we still have to decide on what basis a situation is to be considered unacceptable. Nevertheless, the principle seems to me necessary after the numerous dramas that have cast their shadow over this end of millennium. It also seems to me relatively practicable in those expressions which interest us most here – those involving collective control, in everyone's interest, over the most monstrous deformations of the social system that is being established in the world. It might thus be thought possible, at least in a first stage, to reach minimal agreement on a negative attitude of rejection towards that which is absolutely unacceptable in the world: rejection of extreme poverty, of systematic exploitation of the weakest (especially children), of genocide and wartime massacres, of indiscriminate terrorism, torture, state oppression, subjugation of minorities, or the marketing of goods that kill in large numbers (hard drugs, antipersonnel weapons, etc.). The way to a basic consensus in this area has been shown in the successive declarations on human rights, or in the declaration on economic and social rights, although they still have to be appropriated by living people (a process which Ignacy Sachs sees as the new definition of development[11]) and written into the relevant institutions.

The principle of rejecting the unacceptable is thus an extension of the negative critique of the value system upon which neoliberal modernity is based. We have already described that modernity as ungeneralizable in practice because of the economic, social and ecological impasses to which it leads, but also as morally unacceptable because of certain results which stem from its deepest inner logic, and which it is neither able nor willing to forgo. Let us repeat that the source of these unacceptable results lies not so much in any principle of the market or liberalism per se as in its definition as the *exclusive* criterion for the organization of society; it is not the quest for profit as such which is the problem, but the granting to it of absolute supremacy over any other consideration in economic and social organization.[12] If this is so, the solution cannot lie just with a search for values opposite to the ones underlying neoliberal modernity, since that would result only in the opposite impasses and excesses, as the experience of 'actually existing socialism' in the Soviet bloc tragically demonstrated. We therefore come back to a recognition of the intrinsic *complexity* of human societies: man is not only a consumer, not only labour-power, not only a mind concerned about autonomy or transcendence, not only one member among others of a social group. He is all of these things, and much else besides. There is no simple and homogeneous universal expression of this complexity.

This explains the difficulty of a *positive* quest for the elements of a new system of values – a difficulty visible, for example, in the complex debates on 'social justice' conducted over a quarter of a century by John Rawls,[13] Amartya Sen[14] and others. Here I shall mention only three positive criteria directly linked with the preceding discussion.

The first criterion is *personal liberty*, the crucial demand of the Enlightenment against political or religious absolutism. No one will deny that this value needs to be permanently kept up to date. But liberty should certainly be extended to the relationship of the individual with the economy – people have a right to be more than just *Homo oeconomicus* – and with a totalitarian globalization from which 'there is no longer any place to hide'.[15]

The second criterion is *solidarity*. For liberty can be conceived only in a way that permits liberty for all, and on condition that it does not destroy the social relations and the forms of solidarity that are essential to the survival and cohesion of societies. This is a political problem as old as human communities themselves. For a long time, neoliberal modernity relied on economic growth and the welfare state to keep it within tolerable bounds (in the rich countries, at least), but it has re-appeared and grown considerably worse in recent decades as a result of the exclusive insistence on values of competition and private appro-priation, and a corresponding tendency to reduce the role of public institutions responsible for arbitration and social support. The demand for solidarity cannot be a demand for unrealistic egalitarianism. Faced with the ascendancy of commodities and business, however, it can at least aim for a world in which fewer and fewer people are cast aside as 'redundant' or 'unnecessary'. From this point of view, John Rawls's two principles of social justice are far from commanding unanimous accept-ance, and anyway do not directly yield operational solutions.[16]

The third criterion – and hence the third positive value – is the necessary link between the previous two; it is *responsibility*.[17] It appears here because the individual is free, but also because all other members of society have a right to go on living, and to be equally free. The importance of responsibility has also greatly increased as a result of new technologies and the acceleration of exchange. At the same time as Sen, the philosopher Hans Jonas showed how collective responsibility had radically changed in recent years, and was forcing people to take account of the long-term effects of their actions, particularly with regard to the survival of the earth's ecosystem.[18] This new requirement was both the result of modernity and its antithesis – which says a lot about the difficulty of meeting it.

We must recognize, then, that rejection of the unacceptable and the search for positive requirements of a new value system throw up many different problems for consideration.

First, there are the conditions under which these new values might emerge, so sharply do they conflict with the weight of the tendencies within the present system. Moreover, it is not only hard to see how new values might be put into practice; the problem of their actual content is even wider and more difficult, because they involve a number of questions that no one today seems to find easy to answer. As we

have seen, these questions concern the modern criteria of social justice, but also the foundations – indeed, the very possibility – of a value
system that can be generalized to the whole planet. What leeway would
such a system have to include? What kind of official recognition would
it enjoy? How can one build on a reality in which globalization forci-
bly imposes certain criteria of social organization, some acceptable and
others totally unacceptable? In the name of what – apart from sheer
survival – should everyone recognize certain values relating to money,
work, enrichment, equality, autonomy of decision-making, authority,
nature, and so on?

Obviously, I cannot have the last word on any of this; nor does
anyone today have sufficient authority to settle matters. But I do not
think we can ignore these questions. Do they not once more indicate
the complexity of the world in which we are involved, and of the
economic and social organization it requires?

CHAPTER 13

TOWARDS
ALTERNATIVE POLICIES

[M]anagement of the economy is much more complex than the choices
presented as alternatives would lead one to suppose.

Jean-Paul Fitoussi, *Le Débat interdit*, p. 261.

If we are to focus the political debate on a positive quest for new
forms of development, rather than remaining with a purely negative
critique of modernity, then we are forced to change quite profoundly
our attitude to the running of economies and societies, and the working
out of development strategies. But how, specifically, should we
investigate the requirements for such a change?

It was at the price of a certain abstractness that the general dimensions of this change – conception of economics, values grounding the
social system, content of development – were preliminarily discussed in
Chapters 11 and 12. This abstractness was, in my view, justified by the
risk of impotence that hangs over any analysis which is not systematic
in nature – that is, which does not set out to identify the inner evolutionary logics and the cumulative mechanisms that they generate. But
the *political* argument cannot rest there. We still have to demonstrate, as
far as possible, that the quest is not purely abstract; we still have to
identify its implications for those who inevitably retain the major responsibility for the general interest within this perspective of social
progress – namely, public authorities at various levels. This final chapter
will accordingly explore a few of the paths 'towards alternative policies', where the plural noun corresponds to the requirement of pluralism set out above.

This, no doubt, is the most difficult task. It would appear to be
indispensable. For what is the point of criticizing the present system if
one is incapable of proposing alternative solutions? What is the point of
replacing general considerations with other general considerations if one

cannot translate them into social practice? But the task is also a formidable one. For the existing system draws its strength from the lack of a coherent and immediately available alternative system, and from the difficulty of devising social practices that are sufficiently innovative to shake themselves free of its ascendancy. The elements put forward here are therefore inevitably modest – not a political programme; no more than first steps in a very long journey. They will only offer *examples*, at various levels of generality (which do not exclude the macroeconomic and macrosocial considerations inherent in the approach); but an attempt will also be made to link them to the actually existing conditions of policy elaboration.

Since the themes relate to politics, they are grouped under two kinds of choice: choice of ends and choice of means. As far as possible, the different categories of actors involved in these choices will be identified, but the main role under consideration will be that of public authorities – which is natural, since the argument concerns the general interest. We should bear in mind, however, that neoliberal ideology treats the general interest as a mere aggregation of particular interests mediated by the price system, and therefore rejects out of hand any explicit focus on it.

LESS REDUCTIVE GOALS AND PRIORITIES

It might be suggested that a goal-centred approach to alternative policies again involves a degree of generality that is too remote from practical decisions. But I would argue strongly that this is not the case. At a time when so many societies are being profoundly dislocated (think of Russia, Algeria, most of sub-Saharan Africa, Colombia, some parts of Asia, or even big-city suburbs and much of the youth in the richest countries), when statistics show constant annual rises in world poverty and ecological degradation, when key international conferences break up because they cannot agree on an agenda for trade negotiations, and when public opinion in the privileged countries is itself stirring over abuses of the near-total liberty granted in practice to the large private corporations – at such a profoundly chaotic time, is it not crucially necessary to challenge the goals (and no longer just the organizational forms) of the so-called 'system' that governs our economies, so that we may then redefine the priorities for action?

In my view, this is the perspective in which we should be looking for alternatives to the broad goals imposed by the world system.

Proceeding through the use of examples, let us start with two of the (highly specific) principles of what has been called the 'Washington consensus':[1] that is, of the development strategies recommended by the Bretton Woods institutions and imposed through financial constraints. These principles are *the key role of growth* and *insertion into the world economy*.

Growth

The critical points made above on the subject of growth contain a striking example of the impasses of development policy, and hence of the necessity and difficulty of elaborating concrete alternatives.[2] The growth objective has the appearances of a particularly abstract construction; it might be one useful indicator among others, provided that its real significance is seen as long-term. But that is not the way in which it is used. Nearly always it serves to justify short-term practical decisions and day-to-day economic behaviour: when public authorities invoke the need for renewed growth to defend their immediate policy; when companies make their strategic calculations in terms of productivity, profitability and competitiveness; and even when individuals try to explain their choices relating to work, savings or investments. In this way, a series of short-term objectives are juxtaposed with one another without any attention to their long-term coherence; a process of indefinite growth is sanctified as an absolute priority in one short-term perspective after another, although such a process is neither possible nor desirable in the long term.

It is this absolute priority of growth-rate maximization which must be radically challenged in any quest for alternative policies. Let us imagine what this might mean in a little more detail.

1. In the elaboration of a country's economic policies, the main focus might no longer be on the overall growth rate but on the growth of output in specific areas considered to be priorities in terms of clearly identified needs (housing construction or road-building, for example; or the production of a particular food staple; or an export drive that could have positive effects on employment or the balance of payments). Inevitably, the setting of such priorities would work to the detriment of other sectors, regarded as corresponding to needs that are secondary, perhaps artificial, and anyway not deserving prioritization.

2. This shifting of the priority away from aggregate growth should be seen as favouring not just specific growth objectives but also goals that

are not expressed in terms of growth, or that could even prove anti-thetical to growth. Examples would be: the reduction of income inequalities (even if this has a negative effect on total savings); job creation programmes in sectors of activity that are not necessarily the most profitable or the most likely to see a rise in productivity; non-profit-making programmes to assist the poor or the excluded; the placing of greater value on badly paid tasks held to be socially necessary (social work in France, for instance); a ban on certain products or certain exports (weapons, antipersonnel mines, drugs, tobacco) that are considered socially undesirable, even if they are profitable in terms of income and the balance of payments; or measures to protect natural resources (forest land, the environment), even if this means giving up faster growth of short-term profits.

3. More broadly still, it may be argued that certain general objectives (not only mainly economic ones, as we see from the frequent allusions in current political rhetoric to democracy, autonomy or a minimum level of security) should be pursuable without having their legitimacy challenged by economists or financiers, even though – contrary to what politicians claim to believe – they may incur a cost rather than a benefit in terms of overall growth.

Altogether, these examples suggest that growth is not a necessary and sufficient condition for an answer to the most legitimate aspirations of individuals and groups, whether or not these are linked with the private appropriation of commodities, and whether or not their main dimension is 'economic' (that is, implies an allocation of scarce resources). This is a truism, no doubt, but it has been largely forgotten by most of the people who are responsible for the economy. We must now look at the operational implications.

Who is responsible?

Upon which players, then, does it fall to modify the absolute supremacy of the growth criterion at various levels of economic decision-making? This is a difficult question, in which we encounter one of the most powerful obstacles to change.

   In principle, all the players are concerned. But as it is a question of the general interest, the public authorities are in the front line, facing fire from the positions of neoliberal ideology. Not only does the whole issue assume a redefinition of the role of the state, on which there is hardly any agreement today; it also runs up against major deficiencies in most of the existing state apparatuses.

It therefore falls primarily to public authorities to demystify both the general discourse that reduces development to growth, and day-to-day economic policy decisions. References to growth should no longer be used here except in conjunction with other references – among which the goals mentioned above should have their place. But these references are not purely formal; they have meaning only if they find expression in an explicit (or at least conscious and organized) political will; only if they do not stem simply from an implicit adaptation, however honest, to the pressures of the moment. They can be taken seriously, then, only once they express themselves in actual strategic choices, with all the budgetary and institutional consequences that these entail.

The removal of the sacred aura surrounding growth should also apply at the level of the firm. Of course, we must avoid mixing everything up together. In a market economy, a firm can survive only if it is profitable and competitive; self-serving discourse about 'civic enterprise' should not breed illusions about the room for manoeuvre available to any one such enterprise, nor about the sincerity of the discourse itself. The rules of the market have to be respected by individual enterprises, none of which can unilaterally forgo competitive considerations even for the sake of the general interest. It is therefore mainly up to the institutional defenders of the general interest – that is, public authorities – to legislate new rules that will apply to everyone, and introduce 'from above' the concerns of social justice and quality of life into the market decisions taken by enterprises. Such rules began to develop mainly in the late nineteenth century, in reaction against the excesses of unbridled capitalism, and the intensification of neoliberal globalization in recent decades has not yet been matched by regulation that is capable of tackling the problems it has created. One of the areas requiring most urgent attention in this respect is the obligation of companies to develop proper accounting for the ecological and social costs associated with their activity. But it remains true that changes at the level of institutions cannot provide for everything; it is in the inevitably remaining margins that the appeal to 'citizenship' will retain a real significance – about which enterprises themselves will have to keep asking questions.

Finally, this change of attitude and of priorities will also be necessary at the level of *individuals*, so that they may shake off a conception of prosperity or social advance limited to the accumulation of commodities and incomes. This is above all an ethical problem, in the sense that it mainly involves a greater individual awareness of what is at stake for the community; even if new policies in this area have to be decided by public authorities, they will require at least a minimum of consent on the part of citizens. On the other hand, this greater awareness can be made considerably easier by the presence of certain conditions in the surrounding economy, and therefore by the imposition of new game rules on all players: for example, recognition of each adult person's right to work or, failing that, to a guaranteed subsistence; public protection of other basic rights such as health, education, housing, security and privacy. But again let us bear in mind that the difficulty is not to gain recognition for these rights in theory – who would dare speak out against them? – but to ensure that, whenever required, they do actually outweigh the criteria of growth and profit. The responsibility of individuals and groups, like that of companies, does not disappear as a result of new interventions on the part of public authorities.

International trade

The sphere of international trade lends itself to the same kind of reasoning. It, also, appears at first sight to be too general, too aggregated, too abstract for any specific recommendations to be made. No doubt the political awareness of what international trade means for the ordinary lives of most people increased considerably during the recent debates on measures taken by the WTO or the EU (on hormone-injected beef or genetically modified food, for example), and the events in Seattle in late 1999 even forced the WTO to postpone a new round of talks on trade liberalization. Nevertheless, individuals are scarcely in a position to take action of their own on such issues, except by at least marginally changing their consumption habits or by taking part in collective protests. Companies too – except perhaps the real giants – are largely helpless in the face of issues which, anyway, do not fall within their competence and their margin for manoeuvre.

Once more, then, it is up to (national and international) public authorities to change the rules of the game, to introduce more criteria for decisions on trade, and to accept that the legitimacy of any form of 'protection' in international trade should be measured not by its conformity with an abstract theoretical model but by the character of the social interests it defends. Protection is unacceptable when it defends the conservatism of firms resistant to change; it is perfectly respectable, in principle, when it defends and organizes the survival of a human group, a collective culture, or some natural environmental capital. But the official statutes of the public and private bodies empowered to take decisions in this sphere, as well as the technocracy that governs them outside any democratic control, are evidently a major obstacle to a reorientation of international trade 'doctrine' along these lines. Consequently, there can be little perspective of institutional change without a profound restructuring of the international public apparatus – a restructuring which has often been evoked even in the last couple of decades as a 'second Bretton Woods', although it would have to go well beyond the two organizations associated with that name.

The thinking required to prepare alternative policies on international trade is thus the same as the thinking we have discussed in relation to growth. It is not a question of giving up all growth, or all insertion into international trade; the crucial point is to recognize that these two goals, currently presented as the *nec plus ultra* of the world system, are in reality only means to the ends that each community (including the global community) has to define on the basis of a new political debate. The costs and benefits of expanding international trade, like those of growth, have to be systematically compared with the various collectively defined goals, in so far as these are recognized as legitimate and compatible with the international order: prospects for employment and income; right to autonomy and cultural identity; right to health care; right of the weakest to protection, and in any event to survival; right to maintenance of the ecological heritage, and so on. The rules of the international game must enable these goals to be defended. But this reveals the difficulty of the 'agenda' that needs to be adopted, which points far beyond the kind of straightforward liberalization that favours the most powerful.

INSTRUMENTS TO SERVE
THE GENERAL INTEREST

Let us now turn to some instruments of these alternative policies. It should already be clear that these mainly concern the public authorities, themselves considered as an instrument. But in order to define the role of these authorities, we need to make a number of preliminary points.

What role for public authorities?

First, let us recall that 'public authorities' refers here to *various levels* of decision-making, not only to the national state. Indeed, one of the main problems facing economic policy in the future is to redefine the role of public authorities at an international or global level (the WTO, the Bretton Woods institutions, the European Union, and others).

Second, there can be no new policies unless the *goals* of those policies, and of the public authorities in general, are spelt out. The 'Washington consensus', as we have seen, allows public authorities only a subordinate role in relation to the market. But such a conception quite clearly issues from an ideological bias. Like growth, and like the expansion of international trade, the state is only an instrument serving higher goals; but the market too must be conceived as an instrument serving these same goals. There is no reason to claim a relationship of subordination between these two instruments: state and market. It is their respective goals which can define their relationship with each other – not only in principle, but in the solution of many concrete problems. It remains true, however, that the tracing of the boundary between state and market is itself a problem concerning the general interest, whose solution can be determined only by the legitimate public authorities.

Third, even if explicit reference is made to the goals pursued, and even if it is accepted that there is no uniform rule to define the roles of state and market in different situations, certain instruments of economic theory should be helpful in reaching a 'rational' definition of those roles. Among these instruments, the concept of 'collective' or 'public' goods – that is, goods which are not susceptible to private appropriation in terms of market economics, but benefit a whole community of users (street lighting, for example, or national defence) – has recently gained a reputation for itself in the quest for new forms of international co-operation.[3] We cannot here go into the huge and promising debate that has been developing. But let us simply note that this concept could be usefully – and most rationally – employed to curb the blind vogue for privatization and deregulation, which ends up denying the very existence of any interest that is not purely private. (Some transport corporations, for example, should remain in public hands, or receive public funding, because they produce collective services that do not lend themselves to market profitability.)

Fourth, if the action of national or international public authorities is to be revalued within a general-interest perspective, they must be given the means to mobilize the necessary resources. This will not necessarily mean raising the level of taxation (for waste is all too familiar a phenomenon in the public services). What should be avoided above all, however, is a simplistic and politically biased debate about the public's

supposed 'tolerance thresholds' for community taxes, without any reference to the uses of public funds and the goals of public intervention
(taxes will obviously vary according to whether health and education,
for example, are free of charge or charged at the market rate). Here we
might follow a recent suggestion by Jean-Paul Fitoussi: that the tax
burden should be increased on firms that have become more profitable
through 'globalization', when that process of globalization has itself re-
ceived clear-cut support from the public authorities in the country in
question; the higher taxes would then represent a kind of fair compensation for private profit resulting from public action.[4]

But public resources are not only financial. Although much public
intervention involves direct public spending, and therefore the taxation
of personal income, this is by no means always the case. I am thinking
here of 'institutional' measures – especially those which, in the name of
the general interest, set a normative framework for the activity of private
players and may affect their income levels, but without involving any
actual taxation or public spending. The importance of this institutional
framework has been stressed many times above. We may also say that,
in the conditions of a modern economy, the 'vocation' of public authorities lies mainly in such administrative intervention, rather than
in the direct production of market goods and services.

The institutional framework

The first set of instruments to be considered, then, are institutions.
They are the principal answer to various problems raised above: the
passage from macro-level to micro-level, in particular, but also, more
generally, the relations between an economics of needs and an economics of profit. The institutional framework is especially well suited
for taking us beyond the accumulation of profit as the sole criterion of
social organization – a step whose necessity has been emphasized
throughout.

A meaning of institutions quite broadly accepted today is *rules of the
social game*: the rules which define the rights, privileges and autonomous scope of various players and needs.[5] The market is an institution
in this sense of the term, as are private property and the contractual
rights bound up with it, the currency defined as legal tender, the legal
or customary rules excluding women's domestic labour or children's
labour from monetary remuneration, and so on. The state is also an
institution, of course, invested with the special power (within its rules
of operation) to define other institutions on its territory.

In a society and an economy essentially governed by the rules of the market, only those needs which correspond to the most viable activities in terms of appropriable profit are satisfied. Public services exist, but their existence is subject to their usefulness for market activities. Let us assume, for the sake of argument, that a community decides to take responsibility for new collective needs that are not necessarily positively correlated with the needs of the market; it might wish, for example, to reduce certain gross disparities of income, or to finance the education of poorer children, or to limit the extent of industrial pollution. Such decisions can be taken only by an authority acting in the name of the public interest, and they can be implemented only through institutional measures such as a limitation on private property and the rights associated with it, a progressive income and wealth tax, the passing of new labour legislation, the strengthening of social security provision, the opening of free public schools, or the dictating of certain prices and charges. Or let us assume that the government is aware of the negative effects of tobacco or alcohol consumption on public health, but does not wish to ban their sale; it may then act on the market by means of a special tax, which considerably increases the purchase price of these goods and discourages their consumption. In terms of the guiding role of the price system in a market economy, the intended effect of such a tax may be analysed as the rationalization of private decisions in line with those desired by the public authorities.

In a majority of such cases, the institutional measures do not abolish market laws and criteria; they limit their scope by means of certain rules or complementary actions (such as the transfer of resources) in the name of the public interest. In other cases, the institutional measures reinforce – or, if you like, protectively cordon off – the role of the market. This is what happened, for example, with the GATT negotiations on international trade and the intergovernmental agreements that resulted from them. The practical importance of such measures is obvious enough.

These are basic mechanisms which do not require lengthy explanation; we can see them operating wherever we look in all modern economies. The organization of so-called 'mixed' economies – that is, of virtually all national economies actually in existence – has no other secret than a combination of the roles of state and market, whose proportions may vary within certain limits. Yet this same principle has been denied by certain neoliberal doctrines, on the grounds that it distorts the sacrosanct play of the market. That it does so is perfectly true, of course, but this is a reason for criticism only if one actually considers the market to be sacrosanct; only if one treats as an end what is nothing but a means. Such a position derives neither from the nature of things nor from a divine decree – no human institution can be regarded as sacred – but from the relationship of forces between the interest groups present in the arena. Freedom certainly is one of the desirable pillars of our societies, but it cannot be freedom only for those who own property.

Again, it comes down to political choices. The example of the institutional framework shows once more the conditions that need to be fulfilled for a political debate about choices to be organized: (a) the existence of an authority invested with responsibilities for the interests of the community; (b) the development by that authority of a 'holistic' vision of the interests in play; (c) a method of preparing material for the debate which takes into account not only the apparent situation at the beginning but also the long-term effects, and which therefore requires a kind of planning (we shall return to this later).

Each of these requirements is obviously antinomic to the recommendations of neoliberalism. We should be under no illusion, then, about the scale of the change in perspective that needs to be made.

Macroeconomic and macrofinancial analysis

Another instrument necessary for the emergence of alternative policies is macroeconomic and macrofinancial analysis. The 'orthodox' form of such analysis – the one practised by most international organizations (IMF, World Bank, OECD, European Union), as well as most finance or economics ministries within national governments – needs to be profoundly rethought and transformed, because it produces a seriously biased picture of the reality of economies and societies.

It does not lack arguments in its defence; it even claims to provide a synthesis based upon a few widely accepted indicators (growth and the structure of production, the structure of external trade and the balance of payments, the state of public finances, money and credit, etc.), which results in a standard schema that lends itself to international comparisons, and therefore to homogenized recommendations for economic policies and development policies. Such international homogenization corresponds to the concerns of the dominant players in the globalization process: those who see only advantages in recommending the same stereotyped prescriptions everywhere.

The real questions, however, seem to be of a different order. Who actually benefits from these advantages? What needs to be known in order to judge whether growth, or increased exports, or neoliberal globalization, is or is not an instrument of 'development', in the sense we have proposed here? What do the traditional macroeconomic and macrofinancial analyses tell us from this point of view, and what do they cover up? What presuppositions have to be taken into account in appraising the range – or lack of range – of such analyses? How do they, or might they, integrate medium- to long-term considerations? How do they avoid (or, on the contrary, reinforce) the misunderstandings or obscurities that result from the divorce between the real sphere and the financial sphere? On all these points – and, no doubt, on many others – the most official of analysts are beginning to understand that their accounting instruments are a mirror which distorts reality. At the Davos Forum in 1997, for example, everyone waxed so ecstatic over the statistical 'good health' of the US economy that the Treasury Secretary himself had to calm things down by mentioning the tragic living conditions of a growing section of the population in the United States, especially in the big cities.

Less simplistic methods of analysis have, to be sure, been attempted for a long time now. The UNDP's *Human Development Report*, in particular, has already presented some results, although these are little used in practice, and a huge task of elaboration still lies ahead. If I stress the need for renewal, it is certainly not because I wish to deny the progress already achieved, but because in practice most of the present masters of globalization are satisfied with the existing methods – methods which correspond to their own priorities, facilitate the homogenization they pursue, and allow it to be more easily measured. Once these productivist and homogenizing aims are seen to be socially suicidal, however, the search for different instruments becomes an urgent necessity.

This search involves a considerable programme that cannot be reduced to a few simple measures. But its main priority, if it is to result in alternative policies, must be to bridge the gap which exists between, on the one hand, the data of 'orthodox' macroeconomic and macrofinancial analysis based on the exigencies of the global system (contribution to overall growth, budget equilibrium, balance of trade, monetary stability, international creditworthiness, openness to foreign capital) and, on the other, the data which more directly measure the level and quality of life within the community concerned, the social and political equilibrium, and the ecological viability of the existing conditions.

Taking account of the medium and the long term

The expression that most adequately describes this taking account of the medium and the long term is no longer a fashionable one, although I think it deserves to be rehabilitated in keeping with the new realities. It is the *planning of public policy* and, more generally, the *planning of development*.[6] In this there is no nostalgia for the past, nor any totalitarian blindness. The argument for a new-style planning stems only from our analysis of modernity and globalization: the liberalization and growing role of market forces, the emergence of powerful decision-makers outside state regulation, the increasing collective problems and the need for economic rationality in tackling them. It goes without saying that the scale of such planning will depend upon the essentially *political* choices that each society makes about the responsibilities for the general interest that should be entrusted to public authorities.

The approach that is needed concerns both analysis and action. The analysis should come from a long-term social perspective – or, if you like, from reflection on the future of society. This does not necessarily mean going back to the large-scale exercises in macroeconomic or geopolitical futurology that were fashionable in the 1960s (and still in the 1970s in the field of international relations). The task, more modestly, is to organize a kind of 'watch', which would make it possible to foresee and analyse in advance a number of probable consequences of the currently observable trends in economy and society, so that those who hold public responsibility should not find themselves completely disarmed when those consequences appear. It is not a question of predicting every detail, but rather of selecting and analysing a small number of collective problems – those linked with demography, for example, with the growing scale of social exclusion, the degradation of ecosystems, the concentration of power in certain sectors, the increased pace of urbanization, and so forth.

We might add to this watch function the above-mentioned effort to diversify ways of expressing social needs.

But it is not enough to record and understand; possible answers to the collective problems must also be prepared at the level of action. This will involve comparing the costs and benefits of various options and attaching these to precisely defined categories of beneficiary and victim. It will involve the organization of a political debate about those options that eventually leads to the setting of priorities, and the preparation of a series of measures required for their implementation.

The setting of priorities is essential to this approach, forcing as it does a combination of political choices and economic rationality which the dominant thinking mostly refuses to contemplate.[7] For, contrary to what many politicians seem to think, the challenge of 'prioritization' cannot be taken on board just through a series of empty declarations about such and such a value or objective; it has meaning only if it can resolve potential conflicts between particular values and objectives, by favouring some, renouncing others, and mediating between a variety of specific interests. Work has already been done in this field, of course, but the methods of 'budget choice rationalization' studied in France in the 1960s (or those of the 'Planning, Programming, Budgeting System' in the United States) are hardly in fashion any longer.

We shall not dwell here on the new ways in which the various phases of public action and development might be organized.[8] Suffice it to recall the reason for this requirement, and then to draw the practical consequences for the search for alternative policies.

The reason for this is the inescapable necessity of rigorous rationalization of public decisions, if we are to break with that especially harmful postulate of modernity according to which the market is the only conceivable economic rationality. As for the practical implications, it can be seen that they will inevitably involve some enlargement of public responsibilities. At least two kinds of measures could enable this to take place:

- the attachment of a small team without operational responsibilities to each international public organization and each national government (and even to each of the major governmental departments), whose sole task would be monitoring and social forecasting in its field of competence;
- expansion of work on the annual budget to include perspectives for public action covering a number of years, both in relation to finances and at the institutional (that is, legislative and regulatory) level, and a long-term macroeconomic and macrofinancial framework that would contain in outline (a) the likely major trends of the economy and society, at least in areas where collective problems might be expected to require sizeable public intervention, and (b) the main guidelines for such intervention.

CONCLUSION

Let us first summarize the main suggestions advanced above. It is necessary:

- to challenge the absolute priority given to indefinite growth in current economic policy, by concentrating on a number of particular growth rates rather than the overall growth rate for the economy, and by allowing room for other economic and non-economic objectives even if they prove inconsistent with the maximization of overall growth;
- to challenge the total freedom of international trade, since trade is only one instrument of development among others, and should allow for the protection of legitimate collective interests;
- to re-examine the role of the national and international public authorities in relation to the goals politically assigned to them, so that they can become a simple instrument serving development on an equal footing with the market;
- to explore the paths opened up by the institutional measures through which the public authorities at various levels produce the rules of the social game;
- to study the technical possibility of a kind of macroeconomic analysis that includes better measurement of the exigencies of the global system and the requirements of social progress;
- to develop a new-style planning of public policies and development policy, especially through the establishment of social forecasting units in national and international public bodies, and through the formulation of long-term financial and macroeconomic perspectives at the same time as the annual preparation of the budget.

Debate on the public authorities' role in neoliberal modernity, and the search for the first elements of 'political alternatives' that might bring about the transformation of that modernity, are obviously tasks far too wide and too complex for us to outline here any directly operational proposals. This chapter has done no more than identify some paths for future exploration, and suggest the need for a new perspective all the more different in that the very goals of public intervention – not just its means of action serving the dominant institution of the market – would need to be questioned on behalf of the general interest.

The above suggestions are addressed first of all to those holding public responsibility or involved in research positions, but they also concern companies, associations and individual citizens. For if the complexity of our societies is one of the main reasons for us to think again about its modes of regulation, we have to be consistent and accept that the redefinition of the role of public authorities should itself be put into perspective. Neither public authorities alone, nor market forces alone, nor even a harmonious combination of these two mechanisms – what we have called here the organization of a 'mixed economy' – can be enough to answer the 'triangle' of economic, social and ecological problems facing our societies in the years to come. This seems to be what Alain Touraine had in mind when, drawing on his previous reflections on new social movements, he demanded the right for all individuals and all groups to 'become players' in the organization of our future.[9]

But the social sciences, and especially economics, are still far from capable of responding to such a demand.

GENERAL CONCLUSION

> The mere degree of a society's industrialization or mechanization will be less significant than the measure of its success in providing solutions to the problems of pollution, of resource exhaustion, and of social tension that are at present the unexorcized concomitants of the industrial system. The future may reveal a non-Western answer to a problem that was originally presented to the world by the West.
>
> Arnold Toynbee, *A Study of History*, p. 571.

Let us first recall the main ideas developed in this book.

1. The thoughts on the expansion and globalization of modernity, in refusing to serve a group of particular interests and players, have had the aim of seeking instead to establish the *general interest*. This has been made more difficult than ever by the sway of liberal ideology, however, which holds that the general interest is nothing but the sum of particular interests, and unjustifiably asserts the dominance of economics over all other human concerns. In the face of this fundamentally economistic view, it has been necessary to analyse the logic of the system it upholds but also to consider the problems raised by the relationship between economics and the other components of the general interest and of social progress. In short, an attempt has been made to analyse the present and future of the system, together with the problems it poses for the general interest.

2. Precisely from the point of view of the general interest, however, the consideration of modernity leads to the conclusion that both its present and its future are unacceptable. As regards the present, the diagnosis is overwhelming: modernity does, to be sure, produce 'development' (in the sense of 'progress'), but at the same time it also

produces underdevelopment and misdevelopment. In what might be called its 'neoliberal deviation', it results in numerous contradictions within the 'triangle' of its economic, social and ecological components. Furthermore, today these contradictions seem to be under no one's control, and the quickened pace of globalization is accentuating the insane and alienating aspects of neoliberal modernity. The future is more disturbing still, because of the promises that cannot be kept. An intensification of various contradictions seems probable – our main examples here have concerned growth, inequality and exclusion, international trade and the role of the public authorities, but other problems could be analysed in relation to urbanization, culture, and perhaps even democracy. Finally – and most important of all – modernity has shown itself to be non-generalizable, thereby transforming the hope of development into a false promise except perhaps for a privileged minority.

3. Does this twofold unacceptability of the present and the future mean that we have to give up the very idea of social progress for humanity as a whole? Such is obviously not the position advocated here. The logical and ethical critique of modernity, as well as the demonstration that it cannot be generalized, apply only to the development model dominant today; they only reinforce the necessity of an alternative perspective, a different form of social progress, *another development*. This formula may be expressed more concretely. Whereas the neoliberal approach defines development exclusively in terms of growth performance, exports, monetary stability and macroeconomic and macrofinancial equilibria, the 'other development' we have in mind, though freely defined by the community concerned, will lay more stress on the multiple dimensions of social progress, on justice and protection for the weakest members of society, on the promotion of democracy and the rule of law, and on respect for the long-term requirements of the planetary ecosystem. Not all these aims are in contradiction with the practices of the present system, but their logics and their basic principles are essentially different. It is in this sense that we may consider globalization to be 'resistible' in its present form, and may go on to invent different forms. Such is the perspective underlying all the thinking in this book – thinking which does not propose any magic formulas, of course, but neither does it give up on the question that is inseparable from any critical analysis in this context: *what is to be done?*

4. One of the things that emerge most clearly from our reflections on the present and the future is the need for an overall vision, and for the

construction of an overall perspective. This may seem terribly banal, yet its precise implications have to be understood. An overall vision does not content itself merely with juxtaposing specialist approaches from a number of disciplines: it seeks to understand, through ongoing concrete analysis, why each of the elements in the reality under study forms an inseparable whole together with all the other elements, and can be grasped only in its relationship of interdependence with them. This is the case with relations among the economic, social and ecological dimensions of development, but it must also apply to the precise links between consumer attitudes and a trend towards redundancies in the workforce, or to the contradictions between anti-state views among the public and the recurrent demand for state protection. At a political level, one of the difficulties associated with the domination of neoliberal ideology stems from the fact that an overall vision is no longer held by any player, and that – to repeat Bourdieu's formulation quoted above – 'the major choices in society are not made by anyone'. This makes some reflection on the desirable *levels* of political and economic decision-making (including local decision-making) all the more important, although the process can hardly be said to have begun yet.

5. In this quest, one of the most important characteristics of the proposed analysis is its stress on the growing complexity of the societies of modernity, and therefore of the conditions for their future progress and development. This complexity is ignored in the simplistic propositions of the ruling wisdom, beginning with those of the international financial organizations. It is because of this complexity that we must recognize, formally and definitively, the impossibility of any *single* criterion of development; yet the single criterion of the maximization of profit and power is precisely what is imposed by the system of neoliberal modernity. Instead of this exclusive criterion and model, it has become crucially important to insist on a *pluralist* requirement in relation to conceptions and possible goals of development (as opposed to the single criterion of growth in production for the market, which gives rise to profit), and also to insist on a plurality of means of regulating the economy (market mechanisms can solve some problems efficiently, but not all, and they should be combined in a non-subordinate relationship with other, more collectively inspired mechanisms, key among which is the role of public authorities). Moreover, in the 'triangle' of economic, social and ecological issues, the absolute predominance currently given to market criteria leads to a worsening of collective problems that can be solved only by the institutions of the

community – yet the market objects to the development of such institutions. All these considerations point to the need for political choices about goals, and for formulas involving a mixed economy at the level of means (on both the supply side and the demand side). In any event, they require a profound change in attitudes to development on the part of those who have responsibilities in this area.

6. These are the main requirements if our thinking is to advance along this path.

- We need to recognize the profoundly political, not technocratic, character of the development process. Before any choice of means, it is necessary to choose goals and therefore ways of mediating between the various interests in play; no real development strategy can avoid the question, 'develop what, and for whom?'

- One consequence of this political character – which should therefore be repeated here – is that any real development strategy must be based upon an overall vision of the problems to be solved. Such a vision requires that we try to grasp the deep logic of the systems in operation (as we have constantly endeavoured to do in this work), stepping back to take a long-term historical perspective. It also entails that each specific choice should try to take account of all the other choices (so that growth is considered along with justice, for example, or unemployment along with the struggle against inflation). In any event, neither the overall vision nor the choice of goals is assured by the market approach alone.

- The question of economic rationality is also posed, of course. It concerns both the consistency of the goals among themselves and the consistency of the chosen set of goals with the allocation of scarce resources to achieve them. This requirement of economic rationality, which is broadly respected by market mechanisms, asserts itself with the same force in relation to collective choices outside the market (though perhaps the practical difficulties are greater, because the price mechanism does not play the same role there). It should be stressed, however, that the rules of 'general' economic rationality are not to be confused with the rules of market rationality.

- The preparation of an enlightened political debate, and of an economic rationalization of political choices, requires a major renewal of our intellectual apparatus of concepts, reasoning and theories; this is a crucial task for future 'development research'.

- All these choices as to ends and means, as well as their economic rationalization, require a method for systematically upholding the general interest in collective decisions about development. This is what used to be called development planning. No one believes in it any more, for reasons that are easy enough to identify, but the basic problem obviously remains and new solutions to it will have to be found.

This list of difficulties and requirements may seem disheartening, especially if we bear in mind the rudimentary character of our thinking, our consciousness, our concepts and our means of action. But the pressures of social reality, the depth of the global dramas in this new century and their implications for society, have become much too significant to allow for discouragement and passivity.

What we have learnt in recent years, however, is a certain modesty in discussing social change. The world has grown considerably more complex, ideological promises have become less credible, and the perspectives for political action have somewhat clouded over. We can no longer pose simple alternatives for our societies, such as 'reform or revolution?', because we have learnt both the ineffectuality of reforms and the excessive cost of revolutions in comparison with their results. But this modesty – or, rather, this new realism – essentially concerns the *means* of action for the general interest, which, as we now know, have to be considerably refined and improved. What it must not do is diminish our *goals* of action, our aim of mastering social change in the face of the impasses of modernity.

That leaves the most difficult problem of all: the problem of the location of power, the problem of building a social and political base to support the renewal of our strategies for progress. It raises the need for knowledge, consciousness and morality; for the transcendence of particular interests.

But difficult though the problem is, we cannot afford to overlook it any longer. For the mastery of social progress does not just involve a thirst for power, or a Promethean dream; it has become a condition for the survival of our societies.

NOTES

CHAPTER I

1. This expression is borrowed from the UNRISD (United Nations Research Institute for Social Development), which published a remarkable work with that title as part of the preparations for the Copenhagen social summit in 1995 (UNRISD, 1994).
2. See Dumont, 1977.
3. See all the work of René Girard, but most particularly *La Violence et le sacré*, 1972.
4. See J.K. Galbraith, *The Culture of Contentment*, 1992.

CHAPTER 2

1. UNDP, *Human Development Report 1997*. The 1997 report is the main one quoted here, because its *special focus is on poverty*. The report for 1999 does not contain exact continuations of the statistical series that we have quoted, but of course it does provide more up-to-date figures on 'human development indicators' for the period from 1990 to 1997 (see p. 22). On income and poverty, it calculates worldwide annual average growth of real GDP at 1 per cent per capita, and the growth of consumption at 2.4 per cent. It further notes that 'nearly 1.3 billion people live on less than a dollar a day, and close to 1 billion cannot meet their basic consumption requirements. The share in global income of the richest fifth of the world's people is 74 times that of the poorest fifth.'
2. Ibid., p. 2.
3. These are the main figures for 1997 given in the *Human Development Report 1999* (p. 22):

   • Education: 'Between 1990 and 1997 the adult literacy rate rose from 64% to 76%', but 'in 1997 more than 850 million adults were illiterate. In industrial countries more than 100 million people were functionally illiterate.'
   • Health: 'Around 1.5 billion people are not expected to survive to age 60'; and 'roughly 340 million women are not expected to survive to age 40'; 'more than 800 million people lack access to health services, and 2.6 billion access to basic sanitation'.

- Food: 'Despite rapid population growth, food production per capita increased by nearly 25% during 1990–97. The per capita daily supply of calories rose from less than 2,500 to 2,750, and that of protein from 71 grams to 76.' However, 'about 840 million people are malnourished', and 'the overall consumption of the richest fifth of the world's people is 16 times that of the poorest fifth.'

4. See Mander and Goldsmith, 1996, p. 6.
5. UNDP, *Human Development Report 1997*, p. 3.
6. Ibid., p. 2.
7. UNDP, *Human Development Report 1999*, p. 22.
8. UNRISD, 1994, p. ix.
9. See Ignacio Ramonet, *Géopolitique du chaos*, 1997; his eloquent overview powerfully supports the argument of this chapter.
10. Ibid., p. 86.
11. Ibid., p. 35.
12. According to the *Human Development Report 1999* (p. 22), 'Every year nearly 3 million people die from air pollution – more than 80% of them from indoor air pollution – and more than 5 million die from diarrhoeal diseases caused by water contamination.'

CHAPTER 3

1. Penguin edition, Harmondsworth 1988, p. 28.
2. Quoted in Greider, 1997, ch. 8.
3. For a remarkably clear review of this concept, see F. Vergara, *Introduction aux fondements philosophiques du libéralisme*, 1992.
4. For an overview, see Robert Castel's excellent *Les Métamorphoses de la question sociale*, 1995.
5. Corm, 1993, p. 29.
6. In *The Wealth of Nations* – which first appeared in 1776, and is considered the founding text of economic science – Adam Smith speaks of 'a certain propensity in human nature … to truck, barter, and exchange one thing for another' (Smith, 1961, p. 17).
7. See Karl Polanyi, *The Great Transformation*, 1944.
8. To borrow from the title of Herbert Marcuse's famous book *One Dimensional Man*, first published in 1964.
9. Louis Dumont, *From Mandeville to Marx: The Genesis and Triumph of Economic Ideology*, 1977a; *Homo aequalis. Genèse et épanouissement de l'idéologie économique*, 1977b and 1985.
10. Dumont, 1977a, p. 4.
11. Ibid., pp. 23–4.
12. Dumont, 1977b, p. 132.
13. See Immanuel Wallerstein, *Historical Capitalism*, 1983.

CHAPTER 4

1. Smith, 1961, p. 18.
2. The term 'Pareto optimum' is named after Vilfredo Pareto, who defined its limited import.

3. See Marshall Sahlins's provocative *Stone Age Economics*, 1972.
4. See Dumouchel and Dupuy, 1979, p. 53.
5. The expression comes from an article by Jean-Marie Domenach, which first appeared in *Esprit* in 1967 and was taken up in the title of a book of his in 1973.
6. Weil, 1955, p. 60.
7. See Polanyi, 1944.

CHAPTER 5

1. 'It should come as no surprise if, at the very moment when the power of the productive apparatuses is posing the problem of the reproduction over time of natural environments as a matter of life, economic science – which, whatever may be said, is based upon this logic alone – finds itself particularly lacking in arguments when confronted with the facts. Never in its history has it proved less suited than today to solve, or even to detect, the major problems of the epoch.

   'Vision narrowed down to the spheres of production and exchange prevents it from situating events in their global interconnectedness; all it knows outside its own field are isolated facts' (Passet, 1979, p. 8).
2. See, for example, Ziegler, 1998.
3. See, for example, the classical texts of J.M. Buchanan, 1985, 1987.
4. In *Capitalism, Socialism and Democracy* (1976), for example, Schumpeter writes (p. 287): 'The prime minister in a democracy might be likened to a horseman who is so fully engrossed in trying to keep in the saddle that he cannot plan his ride, or to a general so fully occupied with making sure that his army will accept his orders that he must leave strategy to take care of itself.' See also the economic theory of democracy put forward by Anthony Downs (1957); and various works by Gordon Tullock and other members of the 'public choice' school (especially Tullock, 1971).
5. I have shown elsewhere (Comeliau, 1998) that 'development planning' corresponds to a demand for medium-term policy rationalization, and is therefore still crucially important.

CHAPTER 6

1. See, for example, Daniel Cohen's discussion (Cohen, 1994) of the extent to which these years were an exception in the history of capitalism.
2. One of the most radical pioneering works in this area is Herman Daly, 1977. But we should also mention the Meadows Report to the Club of Rome: *The Limits to Growth*, 1972.
3. See Paul Bairoch, *Victoires et déboires*, 1997, vol. 1.
4. See Heinsohn and Steiger, 1998. I should like to thank Professor Rolf Steppacher, course director at the IUED (Graduate Institute of Development Studies) in Geneva, for drawing my attention to this new work and to its implications for our understanding of the development process.
5. Georgescu-Roegen, 1971, 1995. I should like to thank Jacques Grinevald, course director at the IUED, translator and friend of Nicholas Georgescu-Roegen, for enlightening me as much as he could (any remaining errors are, of course, mine) on certain aspects of this difficult theory. Georgescu's key work (1971) has never been translated into French or indeed republished

in English. In fact it is virtually impossible to find, and one may well think that this is not altogether an accident.

6. Georgescu-Roegen, 1995, p. 115. This is an explicit criticism of the positions of Herman Daly.
7. Ibid., p. 85.
8. Castel, p. 445.
9. *Le Monde*, 25 November 1997.

CHAPTER 7

1. This critique is the starting point for an IUED document jointly authored in the preparations for the Copenhagen Summit: see IUED, 1994.
2. In addition to the last few issues of the UNDP's annual *World Development Report*, see Bairoch, 1997, vol. 3, pp. 536, 1036; Giraud, 1996, drawing on Bairoch's work; also Adelman and Robinson, 1989; Sen, 1992; and the older work of Kuznets (especially *Modern Economic Growth*, 1966).
3. Giraud, 1996, pp. 9–10; Bairoch, 1997.
4. Piketty, 1997; Drèze and Sen, 1995.
5. I have developed this point in an article in *Esprit* (Comeliau, 2000).
6. Mander and Goldsmith, 1996, p. 18.
7. UNDP, 1997, p. 82.
8. Galbraith, 1992.
9. See Guillebaud, 1995, pp. 57ff.

CHAPTER 8

1. As in the title of a work by Robert Castel, 1996.
2. Rifkin, 1996.
3. Méda, 1995.
4. Polanyi, 1944.
5. Rifkin, 1996. See also the cry of indignation – perhaps simplistic to professional ears, but intrinsically legitimate – in Viviane Forrester, *The Economic Horror*, 1999; and the critique of this book in Jacques Généreux, *Une raison d'espérer: L'horreur n'est pas économique, elle est politique*, 2000. Hobsbawm, for his part, wrote in 1994: 'To put it brutally, if the global economy could discard a minority of poor countries as economically uninteresting and irrelevant, it could also do so with the very poor within the borders of any and all its countries, so long as the number of potentially interesting consumers was sufficiently large' (*The Age of Extremes*, p. 573).
6. Greider, 1997, p. 21.
7. Ibid.
8. See the figures on the structure of the economically active population in Bairoch, 1997, vol. 3, pp. 738–44.
9. See, for example, Lesourne, 1997; Piketty, 1997.
10. Lesourne, 1997.
11. Ibid., p. 191.

CHAPTER 9

1. We might recall here the three 'stages' in Fernand Braudel's monumental *Civilization and Capitalism: 15th–18th Century* (1985): the structures of everyday life, the wheels of commerce, and the perspective of the world.

2. Galbraith, 1967.
3. Bairoch, 1994.
4. Rainelli, 1999, p. 86.
5. I borrow this provocative account from the (as yet unpublished) contribution of Susan George to a debate organized in Paris on 24 September 1999 by the International Association of Technicians, Experts and Researchers, on the theme 'Globalization, international financial institutions and sustainable development'.
6. In a widely quoted work, however, Clinton's former Labor Secretary Robert Reich wrote in 1991: 'Rather than increase the profitability of corporations flying its flag, or enlarge the worldwide holdings of its citizens, a nation's economic role is to improve its citizens' standard of living by enhancing the value of what they contribute to the world economy.' See Reich, 1991, p. 301.
7. Reed, 1999.
8. Sen, 1981.

CHAPTER 10

1. For a critique of this approach, see a recent *Cahier de l'IUED* edited by Marc Hufty and bearing the title *La Pensée comptable. État, néo-libéralisme, nouvelle gestion publique* (Hufty, 1998).
2. World Bank, 1993.
3. Comeliau, 1998, in Hufty, *La Pensée comptable*.
4. See *The East Asian Miracle*, World Bank, 1993.
5. Touraine, 1999.
6. Hufty, 1998.
7. Krugman, 1996.
8. Toynbee, 1972.

CHAPTER 11

1. For another analysis that goes in the same direction, see Ramonet, 1997, p. 75.
2. Quite some time ago, I attacked this failure to build on existing results in the case of political economy in Africa. See Comeliau, 1979.
3. On this point, see Généreux, 1997, esp. ch. 6, which sees in it a 'reason to hope'. See also Beaud, 1997, who notes that 'today the most powerful and wealthy societies have no project, so that what count most are the play of social logics and the strategy of the big corporations' (p. 230).

CHAPTER 12

1. For an example of such a historical analysis, see Todd, 1998.
2. Here are a few examples. Which social classes does Galbraith (1992) include in, and which does he exclude from, his 'culture of contentment'? To which bourgeoisie did Tawney limit his 'acquisitive society' in 1920? Who is part of today's 'consumer society', and who recognizes himself or herself in the diffuse ideological 'cult of free enterprise'?
3. See especially Walzer, 1997.

4. The presentation in this section does not relate to any similar text in particular, but I have drawn especially upon the work of Jean-Claude Guillebaud (1995) and two books by Dominique Méda (1998, 1999). I have also found inspiration in Simone Weil's penetrating remarks written in 1934, well before the postwar 'golden age' and the onset of globalization (Weil, 1958). See also Petrella, 1996.

5. As Jean-Claude Guillebaud has pointed out, however (1995, p. 95), the American economist Paul Krugman was already speaking in 1990 of an 'age of diminishing expectations' (Krugman, 1990).

6. Steiner, 1971, p. 29.

7. This expression is suggested by Jean-Claude Guillebaud (1995). In the same perspective, Jacques Généreux writes about the French situation: 'In the 1970s, and up until quite recently, the vast majority of voters had no real interest in an effective struggle against unemployment and poverty; they were not affected by such problems and would still have had to bear the burden of reforms and employment policies' (Généreux, 2000, p. 95).

8. See also Bairoch, 1997, vol. 1, especially his discussion of the reasons why the Industrial Revolution occurred first in Europe rather than elsewhere.

9. On this theme of 'reappropriation', which is constantly invoked by the international financial organizations, see Jean-François Bayart, ed., *La Réinvention du capitalisme* (1994).

10. See the title of Philippe Van Parijs's *Qu'est-ce qu'une société juste?*, 1991.

11. Sachs, 1998.

12. Jacques Généreux writes in this connection: 'It is not against the law of profit that we should take up arms, but against the law of private profit applied to choices in social policy, and so on' (Généreux 2000, p. 55).

13. Rawls, 1972.

14. See especially his *On Ethics and Economics* (1987). Jean-Claude Guillebaud (1999, pp. 283f.) speaks of 'six principles that have to be refounded.... Regained hope instead of abandonment or derision; the defence of equality against domination by the strongest; a rehabilitation of politics against market "inevitabilities"; critical (and modest) reason taken as a thousand times preferable to scientism accompanied with warnings about non-compliance; solidarity and shared convictions as opposed to vindictive individualism; justice in the place of sacrificial vengeance.'

15. Greider, 1997.

16. See Rawls, 1972, section 11. His first proposed formulation of the two principles of social justice is as follows: 'First: each person is to have an equal right to the most extensive basic liberty compatible with a similar liberty for others. Second: social and economic inequalities are to be arranged so that they are both (a) reasonably expected to be to everyone's advantage, and (b) attached to positions and offices open to all' (p. 60).

17. This, it seems to me, is what Amartya Sen has in mind when he insists on a view of individual freedom as social responsibility (Sen, 1987).

18. Jonas, 1984.

CHAPTER 13

1. The term seems to have been coined by John Williamson (1994, 1997). See also the proposal by Joseph Stiglitz, chief economist at the World

Bank until the end of 1999, to move 'beyond' the Washington consensus (Stiglitz, 1998), and the various comments on a lecture given at UNESCO on the theme 'Beyond the Washington Consensus' (see EHESS, 2000).

2. For a good example of the 'trade-off' argument concerning growth and other goals in development strategy, see Raja Chelliah's article on the coming decade in India (Chelliah, 1999).

3. See the recent work published by the UNDP: *Global Public Goods* (Kaul et al., 1999).

4. Fitoussi, 2000.

5. See especially Bromley, 1989.

6. I take the liberty here of referring to my recently published *Planifier le développement: illusion ou réalité?* (Comeliau, 1999).

7. We may find surprising, for example, this peremptory statement made in a recent interview by Pierre-Noël Giraud (a writer hardly to be suspected of blind conformity with the dominant thinking): 'I do think that one can engage in economic discourse only about capitalisms. By this I mean that economic discourse has nothing interesting to say about a tribe in New Guinea, or even – to take a massive example closer to us – about Soviet socialism or socialisms in general' (Giraud, 1999, p. 33).

8. See Comeliau, 1999.

9. Touraine, 1999.

BIBLIOGRAPHY

Adelman, I. and Robinson, S., 'Income Distribution and Development', in Hollis B. Chenery and T.R. Srinivasan (eds), *Handbook of Development Economics*, vol. 2, North Holland, 1989.

Arrous, Jean, *Les Théories de la croissance*, Paris: Seuil, 1999.

Bairoch, Paul, *Economics and World History: Myths and Paradoxes,* New York: Harvester Wheatsheaf, 1993.

Bairoch, Paul, *Victoires et déboires: Histoire économique et sociale du monde: du XVIᵉ siècle à nos jours*, 3 vols, Paris: Gallimard, 1997.

Bayart, Jean-François (ed.), *La Réinvention du capitalisme*, Paris: Karthala, 1994.

Beaud, Michel, *Le Basculement du monde: De la terre, des hommes et du capitalisme*, Paris: La Découverte, 1997.

Behr, Edward, *Une Amérique qui fait peur*, Paris: Plon, 1996.

Bertrand, Maurice, 'Aspects idéologiques du concept de propriété', unpublished, March 1997.

Billeter, Jean-François, 'Regard d'un sinologue sur la Chine d'aujourd'hui', unpublished text of a lecture given at the Geneva Asia Society, 2 June 1999.

Bourdieu, Pierre, *Sur la télévision*, Paris: Liber-Raisons d'agir, 1996/*On Television and Journalism*, London: Pluto, 1998.

Braudel, Fernand, *Civilisation matérielle, économie et capitalisme, XVᵉ–XVIIIᵉ siècle*, 3 vols, Paris: Armand Colin, 1979/*Civilization and Capitalism, 15th–18th Century*, 3 vols, London: Fontana, 1985.

Braudel, Fernand, *La Dynamique du capitalisme*, Paris: Arthaud, 1985; *Afterthoughts on Material Civilization and Capitalism*, Baltimore, MD: Johns Hopkins University Press, 1977.

Bromley, Daniel W., *Economic Interests and Institutions: The Conceptual Foundations of Public Policy*, Cambridge, MA and Oxford: Basil Blackwell, 1989.

Bruttin, Marie-Danièle, *Philosophie politique et justice sociale: Une mise en perspective typologique du débat contemporain autour de John Rawls*, University of Geneva, Département de science politique, *Études et recherches* no. 39, 1999.

Buchanan, James N., *Liberty, Market and State: Political Economy in the 1980s*, New York: New York University Press, 1985.

Buchanan, James N., *Economics: Between Predictive Science and Moral Philosophy*, Texas: A&M University Press, 1987.

Castel, Robert, *Les Métamorphoses de la question sociale: Une chronique du salariat*, Paris: Fayard, 1995.

Chelliah, Raja J., 'Economic Strategy for the Next Decade', *Economic and Political Weekly*, vol. XXXIV, no. 36, 4–10 September 1999, pp. 2582–7.

Cohen, Daniel, *Les Infortunes de la prospérité*, Paris: Julliard, 1994/*The Misfortunes of Prosperity: An Introduction to Modern Political Economy*, Cambridge, MA: MIT Press, 1995.

Comeliau, Christian, 'L'économie politique en Afrique ou les profits d'une mystification', *Canadian Journal of Development Studies/Revue canadienne d'études africaines*, vol. 13, nos 1–2, 1979, pp. 179–94.

Comeliau, Christian, *Les Relations Nord–Sud*, Paris: La Découverte, 1991.

Comeliau, Christian (ed.), *L'Économie à la recherche du développement: Crise d'une théorie, violence d'une pratique*, Geneva: Nouveaux Cahiers de l'IUED, and Paris: PUF, 1996.

Comeliau, Christian, 'L'État subordonné', in Marc Hufty (ed.), *La Pensée comptable: État, néo-liberalisme, nouvelle gestion publique*, Geneva: Nouveaux Cahiers de l'IUED, and Paris: PUF, 1998, pp. 41–56.

Comeliau, Christian, *Planifier le développement: illusion et réalité*, CIDEP, University of Louvain-la-Neuve, 1999.

Comeliau, Christian, 'Pour une coopération privilégiant la lutte contre les inégalités', *Esprit*, June 2000.

Corm, Georges, *Le Nouveau Désordre économique modiale: Aux racines des échecs du développement*, Paris: La Découverte, 1993.

Daly, Herman E., *Steady-State Economics*, Washington, DC: Island Press, 2nd edn with new essays, 1991 (first published 1977).

Domenach, Jean-Marie, *Le Retour du tragique*, Paris: Seuil, 1973.

Downs, Anthony, *An Economic Theory of Democracy*, New York: Harper & Row, 1957.

Drèze, Jean and Sen, Amartya, *India: Economic Development and Social Opportunity*, Oxford: Oxford University Press, 1995.

Dumont, Louis, *From Mandeville to Marx: The Genesis and Triumph of Economic Ideology*, Chicago: University of Chicago Press, 1977a/*Homo aequalis: Genèse et épanouissement de l'idéologie économique*, Paris: Gallimard, 1977b, 1985.

Dumouchel, Paul and Dupuy, Jean-Pierre, *L'Enfer des choses: René Girard et la logique de l'économie*, Paris: Seuil, 1979.

Dupuy, Jean-Pierre, *Le Sacrifice et l'envie: Le libéralisme aux prises avec la justice sociale*, Paris: Calmann-Lévy, 1997.

EHESS, 'The Development Debate: Beyond the Washington Consensus', *International Social Science Journal* 166, December 2000, Blackwell Publishers/UNESCO.

Fitoussi, Jean-Paul, *Le Débat interdit: Monnaie, Europe, pauvreté*, Paris: Arléa, 1995; reprinted Paris: Seuil, 2000.

Fitoussi, Jean-Paul, 'La République et la mondialisation', *Le Monde*, 4 January 2000.

Forrester, Viviane, *L'Horreur économique*, Paris: Fayard, 1996/*The Economic Horror*, Cambridge: Polity Press, 1999.

Galbraith, John Kenneth, *The New Industrial State*, London: Hamish Hamilton, 1967.

Galbraith, John Kenneth, *The Culture of Contentment*, Boston, MA: Houghton Mifflin 1992.

Généreux, Jacques, *Une raison d'espérer. L'Horreur n'est pas économique, elle est politique*, Paris: Plon, 1997, 2000.

Georgescu-Roegen, Nicholas, *The Entropy Law and the Economic Process*, Cambridge, MA: Harvard University Press, 1971.

Georgescu-Roegen, Nicholas, *Energy and Economic Myths*, New York: Pergamon, 1977.

Georgescu-Roegen, Nicholas, *La Décroissance: Entropie, écologie, économie*, Paris: Sang de la Terre, 1979.

Girard, René, *La Violence et le sacré*, Paris: Grasset, 1972.

Giraud, Pierre-Noël, *L'Inégalité du monde: Économie du monde contemporain*, Paris: Gallimard, 1996.

Giraud, Pierre-Noël, *Économie, le grand Satan?*, interview with Philippe Petit and Thérèse Giraud, Paris: Éditions Textuel, 1998.

Gorz, André, *Métamorphoses du travail, quête du sens: Critique de la raison économique*, Paris: Galilée, 1988/*Critique of Economic Reason*, London: Verso, 1989.

Gorz, André, *Misères du présent, richesse du possible*, Paris: Galilée, 1997.

Greider, William, *One World, Ready or Not: The Maniac Logic of Global Capitalism*, New York: Simon & Schuster, 1997.

Guillebaud, Jean-Claude, *La Trahison des Lumières: Enquête sur le désarroi contemporain*, Paris: Seuil, 1995.

Guillebaud, Jean-Claude, *La Tyrannie du plaisir*, Paris: Seuil, 1998/*The Tyranny of Pleasure*, New York: Algora, 1999.

Guillebaud, Jean-Claude, *La Refondation du monde*, Paris: Seuil, 1999/*Refounding the World: A Western Testament*, New York: Algora, 2001.

Heinsohn, Gunnar and Steiger, Otto, 'Alternative Theories of the Rate of Interest: A Reconsideration', mimeo, University of Bremen, 1998.

Hobsbawm, Eric J., *The Age of Extremes: The Short Twentieth Century, 1914–1991*, London: Abacus, 1995.

Hufty, Marc (ed.), *La Pensée comptable: État, néo-liberalisme, nouvelle gestion publique*, Geneva: Nouveaux Cahiers de l'IUED and Paris: PUF, 1996.

IUED, *Pour un développement social différent: Recherche d'une méthode d'approche*, rapport d'un groupe de travail en vue de la Conférence des nations unies sur le dévelopement social, March 1995, Copenhagen, Graduate Institute of Development Studies, Geneva, 1994.

Jonas, Hans, *The Imperative of Responsibility: In Search of an Ethics for the Technological Age*, Chicago: University of Chicago Press, 1984.

Kaul, Inge, Grundeberg, Isabelle and Stern, Marc A., *Global Public Goods: International Competition in the 21st Century*, New York and Oxford: UNDP/Oxford University Press, 1999.

Krugman, Paul R., *The Age of Diminishing Expectations*, Cambridge, MA: MIT Press, 1990.

Krugman, Paul R., *Pop Internationalism*, Cambridge, MA: MIT Press, 1996.

Kuznets, Simon, *Modern Economic Growth: Rate, Structure and Spread*, New Haven and London: Yale University Press, 1966.

Labarde, Philippe and Maris, Bernard, *Ah Dieu! Que la guerre économique est jolie!*, Paris: Albin Michel, 1998.

Lesourne, Jacques, *Vérités et mensonges sur le chomâge*, Paris: Odile Jacob, 1997.

Mander, Jeremy and Goldsmith, Edward (eds), *The Case against the Global Economy and for a Turn toward the Local*, San Francisco: Sierra Club Books, 1996.

Marcuse, Herbert, *One Dimensional Man*, London: Routledge & Kegan Paul, 1964.

Marshall, Alfred, *Principles of Economics: An Introductory Volume*, 8th edn, London: Macmillan, 1964.

Meadows, Donella H., Meadows, Dennis L., Randers, Jorgen, and Behrens, William W., *The Limits to Growth: A Report for the Club of Rome's Project on the Predicament of Mankind*, Washington, DC: A Potomac Associate Book, 1972.

Méda, Dominique, *Le Travail, une valeur en voie de disparition*, Paris: Aubier, 1995; 2nd edn Paris: Flammarion, 1998.

Méda, Dominique, *Qu'est-ce que la richesse?*, Paris: Aubier, 1999.

Musgrave, Richard A. and Peacock, Alan T. (eds), *Classics in the Theory of Public Finance*, London: Macmillan, 1967.

Observatoire de la mondialisation, *Lumière sur l'AMI*, Paris: L'Esprit frappeur, 1998.

Passet, René, *L'Économique et le vivant*, Paris: Payot, 1979.

Petrella, Riccardo, *Le Bien commun: Éloge de la solidarité*, Brussels: Éd. Labor, 1996.

Piketty, Thomas, *L'Économie des inégalités*, Paris: La Découverte, 1997.

Polanyi, Karl, *The Great Transformation: The Political and Economic Origins of Our Time* (1944), Boston, MA: Beacon Press, 1957.

Rainelli, Michel: *L'Organisation mondiale du commerce*, Paris: La Découverte, 4th edn, 1999.

Ramonet, Ignacio, *Géopolitique du chaos*, Paris: Galilée, 1997.

Rawls, John, *A Theory of Justice*, Cambridge, MA: Harvard University Press, 1972.

Reed, David, 'Globalization, the Hegemon, and Environmental Scarcity' (first draft), Geneva: Graduate Institute of Development Studies, June 1999.

Reich, Robert, *The Work of Nations: Preparing Ourselves for 21st-Century Capitalism*, London: Simon & Schuster, 1991.

Rifkin, Jeremy, *La Fin du travail*, with a preface by Michel Rocard, Paris: La Découverte, 1996.

Sachs, Ignacy, 'Le développement en tant qu'appropriation des droits de l'homme', *Estudos Avançados*, 1998.

Sahlins, Marshall, *Stone Age Economics*, Chicago: Aldine Atherton, 1972.

Schumpeter, Joseph, *Capitalism, Socialism and Democracy*, 5th edn, London: George Allen & Unwin, 1976.

Sen, Amartya, *Poverty and Famines: An Essay on Entitlement and Deprivation*, Oxford: Clarendon Press, 1981.

Sen, Amartya, *On Ethics and Economics*, Oxford: Basil Blackwell, 1987.

Sen, Amartya, *Inequality Reexamined*, Oxford: Clarendon Press, 1992.

Smith, Adam, *The Wealth of Nations*, London: Methuen, 1961.

Steiner, George, *In Bluebeard's Castle: Some Notes towards the Redefinition of Culture*, London: Faber, 1971.

Stiglitz, Joseph, *More Instruments and Broader Goals: Moving towards the Post-Washington Consensus*, WIDER Annual Lecture, World Institute for Development Economics Research, January 1998.

Stiglitz, Joseph, *Towards a New Paradigm for Development: Strategies, Policies and Processes*, Prebisch Lecture at UNCTAD, Geneva, 19 October 1998.

Tawney, R.H., *The Acquisitive Society* (1920), New York: Harvest Books, 1948.

Todd, Emmanuel, *L'Illusion économique: Essai sur la stagnation des sociétés développées*, Paris: Gallimard, 1998.

Touraine, Alain, *L'Après-socialisme*, Paris: Grasset, 1980.

Touraine, Alain, *Critique de la modernité*, Paris: Fayard, 1992/*Critique of Modernity*, Oxford: Blackwell, 1995.

Touraine, Alain, *Comment sortir du libéralisme?*, Paris: Fayard, 1999.

Toynbee, Arnold J., *A Study of History*, new revised and abridged edn, Oxford: Oxford University Press, 1972.

Tullock, Gordon, 'Public Decisions as Public Goods', *Journal of Political Economy*, vol. LXXIX, no. 4, July–August 1971, pp. 913–18.

UNDP (United Nations Development Programme), *Human Development Report*, annual, Oxford: Oxford University Press.

UNRISD (United Nations Research Institute for Social Development), *État de désarroi: Les répercussions sociales de la mondialisation*, rapport de l'UNRISD pour le sommet mondial sur le développement social, London: Banson, 1995.

Van Parijs, Philippe, *Qu'est-ce qu'une société juste? Introduction à la pratique de la philosophie pratique*, Paris: Seuil, 1991.

Vergara, Francisco, *Introduction aux fondements philosophiques du libéralisme*, Paris: La Découverte, 1992.

Wallerstein, Immanuel, *Historical Capitalism*, London: Verso, 1983.

Walzer, Michael, *Pluralisme et démocratie*, Paris: Esprit, 1997.

Weil, Simone, *Réflexions sur les causes de la liberté et de l'oppression sociale*, Paris: Gallimard, 1955/*Oppression and Liberty*, London: Routledge & Kegan Paul, 1958.

Williamson, John (ed.), *The Political Economy of Reform*, Washington, DC: Institute for International Economics, 1994.

Williamson, John, 'The Washington Consensus Revisited', in Louis Emmerij (ed.), *Economic and Social Development into the XXI Century*, Washington, DC: Inter-American Development Bank, 1997, pp. 48–61.

World Bank, *The East Asian Miracle: Economic Growth and Public Policy*, A World Bank Research Report, published for the World Bank, Oxford: Oxford University Press, 1993.

Ziegler, Jean, *Les Seigneurs du crime: Les nouvelles mafias contre la démocratie*, Paris: Seuil, 1998.

INDEX

Zed Titles on the Political Economy of Capitalism

Intellectual fashion continues to prompt changes in vocabulary. Today, globalization and the market have become the dominant buzzwords. In reality, however, what is happening is an ongoing, perhaps accelerating, spread (as well as transformation) of the market nexus between members of society on the one hand and relations of exploitation of labour on the other. Whatever terms different writers use, the world's economic systems are, with the collapse of the socialist project, almost exclusively capitalist and the political economy of capitalism remains a centrally important focus of social understanding. Zed Books has a strong list of titles in this area.

N.A. Adams, *Worlds Apart: The North–South Divide and the International System*

Samir Amin: *Capitalism in The Age of Globalization: The Management of Contemporary Society*

Asoka Bandarage: Women, *Population and Global Crisis: A Political-Economic Analysis*

Robert Biel, *The New Imperialism: Crisis and Contradictions in North–South Relations*

Walden Bello, Nicola Bullard and Kamal Malhotra (eds), *Global Finance: New Thinking on Regulating Speculative Capital Markets*

Peter Custers, *Capital Accumulation and Womens Labour in Asian Economies*

Diplab Dasgupta, *Structural Adjustment, Global Trade and the New Political Economy of Development*

W. Dierckxsens, *The Limits of Capitalism: An Approach to Globalization without Neoliberalism*

Graham Dunkley, *The Free Trade Adventure: The WTO, the Uruguay Round and Globalism: A Critique*

Terence Hopkins and Immanuel Wallerstein et al., *The Age of Transition: Trajectory of the World-System, 1945-2025*

Jomo K.S., *Tigers in Trouble: Financial Governance, Liberalization and the Crises in East Asia*

Steve Keen, *Debunking Economics: The Naked Emperor of the Social Sciences*

Joel Kovel, *The Enemy of Nature*

Serge Latouche, *In the Wake of the Affluent Society: An Exploration of Post-Development*

Arthur MacEwan, *Neoliberalism or Democracy? Economic Strategy, Markets and the Alternatives for the 21st Century*

John Madeley, *Big Business, Poor Peoples: The Impact of Transnational Corporations on the World's Poor*

John Mihevic, *The Market Tells Them So: The World Bank and Economic Fundamentalism in Africa*

Saral Sarkar, *Eco-Socialism or Eco-Capitalism? A Critical Analysis of Humanity's Fundamental Choices*

Hans-Peter Martin and Harald Schumann, *The Global Trap: Globalization and the Assault on Prosperity and Democracy*

James Petras and Henry Veltmeyer, *Globalization Unmasked: Imperialism in the 21st Century*

Harry Shutt, *The Trouble with Capitalism: An Enquiry into the Causes of Global Economic Failure*

Kavaljit Singh: *The Globalization of Finance: A Citizens' Guide*

Kavaljit Singh, *Taming Global Financial Flows: Challenges and Alternatives in the Era of Financial Globalization*

Bob Sutcliffe, *100 Ways of Seeing an Unequal World*

Oscar Ugarteche, *The False Dilemma: Globalization Opportunity or Threat?*

David Woodward, *Foreign Direct and Equity Investment in Developing Countries: The Next Crisis?*

For full details of this list and Zed's other subject and general catalogues, please write to: The Marketing Department, Zed Books, 7 Cynthia Street, London N1 9JF, UK or email Sales@zedbooks.demon.co.uk. Visit our website at: http://www.zedbooks.demon.co.uk.